GOD
IS
RICE

Masao Takenaka

GOD IS RICE

Asian culture and Christian faith

THE **RISK** BOOK SERIES

World Council of Churches, Geneva

Cover design: Rob Lucas

ISBN 2-8254-0854-9

© 1986 World Council of Churches, 150 route de Ferney,
1211 Geneva 20, Switzerland

No. 30 in the Risk book series

Printed in Switzerland

Table of contents

Introduction

Brought together here are four lectures which I have given in recent years. In all of them I reflect on Japanese culture in the light of the Christian faith. The first three were the Earl Lectures which I gave in January 1985, at the invitation of the Pacific School of Religion. The last lecture was given at Diana Pura in Bali, Indonesia, at a consultation on "Theology and Culture" sponsored by the Reformed Church in Indonesia in March 1985. I would like to express my sincere gratitude to both these organizations.

Together with many Asian colleagues I have been trying to grapple with the meaning of Christian faith in the Asian social and cultural context.

Between 1959 and 1973 I was involved in urban and industrial mission in Asia. Those were the days of nation-building. It was a time of rapid social change in Asian countries. When the EACC (East Asia Christian Conference, now CCA, Christian Conference of Asia) was inaugurated in 1959, I was asked to be chairman of the Committee on the Witness of the Laity in which industrial mission was located, along with rural mission and medical mission.

The basic commitment of the churches in Asia at that time was expressed through the words of D.T. Niles in terms of the selfhood of the church.[1] The venue of the inaugural assembly of the East Asia Christian Conference signified the spirit of the time. It was Kuala Lumpur, the capital of the newly independent state of Malaysia.

Most Asian countries had attained political independence by then, and were involved in the demanding task of nation-building. Christians in Asian countries were small minority groups, formed for the most part by the missionary movement during the colonial period. They were now for the first time together under the guidance of the Holy Spirit to form a community of common witness

---

[1] See *Upon the Earth*, London, Lutterworth Press, 1962.

2

and joint action, breaking out of the bondage of colonial-
ism and missionary domination. Thus, the selfhood of the
church was emphasized at a time when the Asian nations
were rediscovering their own selfhood.

As we look back and read anew the documents that
came from Kuala Lumpur 1959, we note the following
four emphases.

First, the note of overwhelming joy in the new-found
fellowship of faith among Asian churches. The message
from the first assembly of the EACC to its member
churches and councils states:

> Every church has gifts which others need, and everyone
> needs what others can give. The Asian churches are learning
> to live in this pattern of common sharing, and we believe that
> our meeting here will strengthen these bonds and open up
> new ways of mutual helpfulness.[2]

It was the first time in history that the churches in Asia were
forming a horizontal fellowship, recovering the selfhood of
each church and entering into an I-Thou relationship with
other churches, including the churches in the West.

The second emphasis was the emphasis on God's
people in an Asian context. Around that time there was an
ecumenical reaffirmation of the ministry of the laity, the
people of God called to witness and serve in every part of
the social, economic, and political life of their nations.
After emphasizing the fact that Christians are ambassadors
sent into the world as God's representatives in the world,
the message of the inaugural assembly stated:

> This means that Christian people must go into every part
> of the life of our peoples: into politics, into social and
> national service, into the world of art and culture, to work in
> real partnership with non-Christians, and to be witnesses for
> Christ in all these realms.

[2] *Witnesses Together*, ed. U. Kyaw Than, official report of the inaugural
assembly of East Asia Christian Conference, May 1959.

The third important emphasis at Kuala Lumpur was on Christian participation in nation-building. The chief spokesman on this subject was M.M. Thomas. Recognizing the positive role of nationalism, M.M. Thomas affirmed that "these struggles to build new political, economic, and social structures and institutions" were what he meant by nation-building, and that these constituted "the basic urge of nationalism in Asia today".

The fourth emphasis was related to the mission of the church. It underlined the church's role as a *creative* rather than as an isolated minority. It stressed the need for involvement in the world rather than withdrawal from the world. D.T. Niles pointed out that the temptation to become a ghetto was strong, and that it was a greater danger than syncretism. M.M. Thomas stressed the importance of the role of Christian intellectuals in the process of nation-building.

The churches in Asia have in various ways tried to follow the guidelines set in Kuala Lumpur. But this historical journey was to reveal in turn different dimensions of the challenging Asian reality. During the last 25 years, the course of Asian history has changed drastically. Some of the changes were anticipated, but some were not entirely expected. What then are the issues we face today?

First of all, in regard to the issue of unity, we have come to see it in the perspective of an embracing wholeness, not only a unity among Asian Christians, but a unity of the human community; and not only a unity of the human species, but also a unity of the whole creation. I believe this is a basic biblical insight.

Paul tells us that "the creation waits with eager longing for the revealing of the children of God" (Rom. 8:19). The early church witnessed to the sovereignty of Christ over all creation, as when Paul writes: "He is the first-born of all creation; for in him all things were created, in heaven and on earth, visible and invisible, whether thrones or dominions or principalities or authorities — all things were created through him and for him" (Col. 1:15-16). This embracing wholeness is also reflected in the Book of Revelation which projects the eschatological vision in terms of seeing "a new heaven and a new earth; for the first heaven and the first earth had passed away".

Another challenge we face in Asia is that of appreciating the potential of people. God's own concern for people is vividly described in passages like this:

> He will dwell with them, and they shall be his people, and God himself will be with them; he will wipe away every tear from their eyes, and death shall be no more, for the former things have passed away (Rev. 21:3-4).

In the last twenty-five years the people in Asia have shed a lot of tears. They have suffered under dictatorial regimes. They have lived in poverty and constantly faced the threat of death. They have suffered under the martial law.

The earlier period was the period of struggle to gain independence from the yoke of colonial rule. Now the situation is more complicated. National autocratic rulers, backed by the military and supported by international political and economic powers, suppress the people in many countries. But the people have become more and more conscious of their plight and their rights; they want to free themselves from such systems of domination.

"People power" in the Philippines made big news in February 1986. It is becoming a force to reckon with in other countries as well. People's power is not just in terms of numbers; it consists in the very fact of people, each person created in God's image for creative participation and responsible mutuality.

We do not mean to idealize people as such. They are vulnerable and weak.

We should not absolutize people's power. But we need to recognize that in their very weakness and powerlessness, they can awaken to their selfhood and participate in the process of recovering the wholeness of all humanity.

We recognize in the biblical drama the special attention given to the recovery of humanity among those who are poor, suffering, and despised. We still emphasize the ministry of God's people in the world, but at the same time we realize that this ministry should be performed within the whole process of the humanization of suppressed people in Asia.

In many parts of Asia we see the awakening of people whose rights were denied for a long time. In Japan we witness the struggle for liberation of the Buraku (discriminated) people, Koreans, and Ainu people. In India, Sri Lanka and many other parts of Asia we see similar movements for liberation by marginalized sections.

The emphasis on nation-building had a development orientation; its initial goal was economic growth, indicated by the GNP; or it concentrated on developing the political and military power of nations. Increasingly development itself has become less concerned with people as people. We know today that even the development of infrastructures, such as bridges, roads, and sewage, which are related to the lives of the people at the grassroots, becomes self-defeating when it does not take place within a framework of people's participation.

One of the rich resources of Asian people is their culture. Many Asian cultures are closely related to nature and rooted in the Asian religions. People do not exist in isolation. They are rooted in a particular soil surrounded by a natural and social environment.

Increasingly in our recent historical journey we have discovered the significance of the cultural resources of the peoples in Asia. Not that we idealize any particular culture. We must be self-critical of our own cultural traditions, and we need to be critical of other cultures as well. But we take our culture seriously because it is the context of our life and determines its character; it is also an instrument by which we interpret and express our Christian faith.

This is another issue we face today — the issue of faith and culture. The Christian attitude towards Asian cultures, like the Christian attitude to any culture, should be dialectical. On the one hand, in the light of the gospel we should be critical of the limitations and negative aspects of our cultural traditions; on the other we should be prepared to interpret and express the Christian gospel in and through our cultural context.

This double process actually has gone on throughout the history of the church. There were rich interactions between the Christian gospel and Western culture. In Asia, we are only beginning to seek, with conscious effort, to be Japanese Christians in a Japanese cultural context, Indian Christians in an Indian cultural context, and Chinese Christians in a Chinese cultural context. This book is a humble attempt to contribute to this effort, from a mainly Japanese perspective.

When he was in his mid-teens Sadao Watanabe, a well-known Japanese print artist, first visited a Christian church, introduced by a neighbour who was a school teacher. He had lost his father when he was ten years old, and tended to live a closed and isolated life. He described his first impression of Christianity as follows:

> In the beginning I had a negative reaction to Christianity. The atmosphere was full of "the smell of butter", so foreign to the ordinary Japanese.[3]

---

[3] "Sadao Watanabe — the Man and His Work", by Masao Takenaka, in *Biblical Prints by Sadao Watanabe*, 1986.

Now in his print work he joyfully depicts the celebration of the holy communion with *sushi*, pickled fish and rice, a typical Japanese dish, served on traditional folk art plates. For him rice is a more natural and a more fitting symbol of daily food than bread which is foreign.

The message of the incarnation is universal but the way in which this is expressed should be uniquely local. "The word became flesh and dwelt among us, full of grace and truth" (John 1:14). The fullness of grace and truth needs to become manifest in the communities of people, each with its own local culture.

Masao Takenaka
Kyoto, Japan

1. God is Rice

The "ha-hah" approach

Let me begin with a note on the approach I am going to take.

During the last ten years or so I have come to recognize more and more the significance of the fact that Jesus spoke of the reality of the kingdom of God in parables. Those who had eyes did not see and those who had ears did not listen. "Their eyes they have closed and their ears are too heavy to hear" (Matt. 13:15).

We live an increasingly hectic life and we are busy with much business. The character for busy in Chinese writing 忙, which Koreans and Japanese also use, literally means to destroy one's heart. If we are too busy, we forget what is most important. It is interesting that the same components of the character for busy 忙 are used to indicate forgetfulness 忘. Both mean the destruction of one's heart.

One of the strange trends in theology is the attempt to develop a rational argument about God. Here I see the strong influence of Greek philosophy on Western Christianity. Whenever two or three Western theologians are gathered together, there is argumentation about God. Like a theological "ya-ya chanbara"[1] they debate about God by saying, I argue.

To argue involves the idea of destroying the concept of the opponent by rational debate. To be sure, we need constantly to use our reason and make our thinking rationally coherent. So often we allow emotion to fragment and distort our thought. But an understanding of God and proof of God's existence cannot be acquired through the ya-ya approach, the approach of rational argumentation.

The Hebrew mind did not work that way. When the Bible says Adam knew Eve, it does not mean Adam

---

[1] See page 71.

acquired a lot of data concerning a woman called Eve, or that he arrived at a rational definition or concept of Eve. It means Adam loved Eve, and they became united, physically and spiritually, as whole people. In order to discern the reality of God which is the task of theology, we need to strengthen the ha-hah approach. That is to say, we must awaken in ourselves an appreciation of the living reality who is God. In the Bible we have many surprising acknowledgments: "Ha-hah! In this way, God is working in our world, in a way I did not know."

Consider the different approaches we have when we look at the moon. The expression "the man in the moon" especially in German, indicates the state of a man who is living in isolation and has no relational existence. When we reach the age of the space shuttle, we are sure to say to ourselves: "When can I go there? And how much will it cost?" This is the approach of enquiry. The moon now becomes the object of calculation. The Japanese think of the moon not as a cold object without an intimate relationship, nor as an object to exploit or conquer, but as a personal companion. One of the ancient poems by Myoe (1173-1232) well expresses the Japanese attitude towards the moon.

> I shall go behind the mountain.
> Go there too, moon also
> Night after night we shall keep each other company.[2]

I believe Jesus had a similar personal relationship with nature. "Consider the flowers of the field, how they grow; they neither toil nor spin; yet I tell you, even Solomon in all his glory was not arrayed like one of these" (Matt. 6:28-29). This is not the ya-ya approach; here is no dissection of the flower, and no metaphysical concept of

---

[2] Yasunari Kawabata, *Japan the Beautiful and Myself*, translated by Edward G. Seidensticker, 1969.

God. What we have is the ha-hah approach to awaken the minds of people to the living reality of God and God's work in the world.

My guru, H. Richard Niebuhr, used to remind us of this appreciative attitude towards reality. He used to say: "Wait a moment!" or "What's going on?" According to C.S. Lewis, when we go down a smooth slope without seeing any signpost, it is the time when the devil smiles.[3]

Atmosphere

Why do I want to use the term "atmosphere" in a theological discussion?

I was born in Beijing, China, and brought up in the north-east of China. When I was ten years old, our family moved back to Japan. I still remember the kind of atmosphere I experienced when I first arrived by boat at the port of Shimonoseki in the western part of Japan. It was early July, still the rainy season. A kind of mist surrounded the skirt of the low mountains overlooking the port. It was very different from the wide-open, dry continent I had left behind. Everything was so small: people, houses, cars and streets. And it was crowded. A tiny space which contained a peculiar air, an atmosphere.

I lived in the Study Center of World Religions at Harvard for a year. There were some twenty families (and a few single people) living there. They held different religious views. They came from different countries, but they were all living together. As we visited one another, although the rooms were similar and the physical environment was very much the same, we instinctively grasped the entirely unique atmosphere of each home. Of course there were the smells of various indigenous ingredients for cooking, like Indian curry, Korean kimchi, and Japanese soya bean sauce, and the different

---

[3] C.S. Lewis, *The Screwtape Letters*, London, G. Bles, 1946.

languages. But there were also unique paintings and prints, different perceptions of social and political concerns, and different religious expressions. The atmosphere changed from home to home.

There are spirits moving and interacting with one another in the whole cosmos, in nature and among human beings, constituting and promoting an atmosphere.

I believe human beings are acutely alert to the atmosphere in which they find themselves. Although it is a very important part, language is only one aspect of the atmosphere. Which shows the limitation of ya-ya theology, the rational, argumentative approach to God.

Professor Toyomune Minamoto, the distinguished scholar of the history of Japanese art, depicts the characteristics of Japanese art in terms of the art of atmosphere. For instance, the art of the tea ceremony is an art of atmosphere. In a small room we touch, through the skin of the whole body, the air, permeated and produced by a fitting appreciation of the gifts of time and season, a harmonious companionship with nature and people, and a simple, yet symbolic, expression of beauty in the instruments used in the tea ceremony and in the scroll painting on the wall. The noise of the kettle as the water boils and even the occasional noise made by the carp as they jump in the nearby pool become a kind of background music.

I believe one of the tragedies of our hectic urban life, with its noise and pollution, is the increasing loss of the art of atmosphere. The question is not how we may occupy the space, it is how we may cultivate the appreciative mind to fill the air with the spirit of peace and justice.

As a concrete example of the ha-hah approach, I would like to refer to the story connected with the Japanese translation of *Light from the Ancient Past: the Archaeological Background of Judaism and Christianity* by Prof. Jack Finegan (1946), formerly a professor at the

Pacific School of Religion. The book was translated by
Prince Takahito Mikasa, a younger brother of Emperor
Hirohito, and published in 1955. How did Prince Mikasa
become interested in translating a book dealing with the
background of the Bible?[4]

Prince Mikasa has now published a book *Ancient
Oriental History and Myself*, in which he explains why he
was interested in the study of ancient Oriental history.
During the war, while he was in China as an army officer,
he had two moving experiences. One was that wherever
he went, even in the remotest parts of China, he saw
something of the work of missionaries. He was convinced
that the Japanese, his own people, were a delightful
people, but it seemed to him that they worked only to
further their own interests. Prince Mikasa wondered what
made these missionaries come to China, far away from
home. There was little they got out of it by way of honour
or profit or acknowledgment. What made them choose
this path of dedication and service?

Later, when he encountered the Red Army, he was
impressed to see how disciplined the soldiers were. They
were particularly committed to the protection of women
and children in the villages. He noticed very little
evidence of stealing or raping. He knew Japanese soldiers
were also disciplined, but it was a strictly military
discipline. They could fight and win battles, but they were
not concerned over the welfare of women and children in
foreign lands. He wondered why the communist soldiers
were more disciplined than the nationalist soldiers led by
Chiang Kai Shek.

These two concrete experiences — meeting dedicated
missionaries in remote parts of China and seeing the

---

[4] In fact he also translated two other books by Jack Finegan, namely,
Handbook of Biblical Archaeology, 1967, and *Archaeology from the Ancient
History of the Orient*, 1983.

disciplined conduct of communist soldiers — led Prince Mikasa to study the historical background of Judaism and Christianity and to translate·three books by Prof. Finegan into Japanese. There was a change in his orientation of life, from traditional Japanese nationalism to biblical humanism, and it was brought about not by the ya-ya debate but by the ha-hah experience in his personal pilgrimage.

Four dimensions of atmosphere

As we know, atmosphere is the air surrounding the earth. One calls to mind a Japanese hillside village enveloped in mist. Or one thinks of a small tea house with a simple single flower-and-scroll painting (for decoration) and the steaming tea kettle in the *irori*, the charcoal fire-place, and the fragrance of the green tea — all interconnected in the minds of those who have come to participate in the tea ceremony. One tends to recall a psychological mood when one thinks of atmosphere.

Atmosphere indicates the whole spirit of the environment that surrounds us. In it we live. To understand what it means, we must think of it as a whole.

First of all, there is the air, given and not made. It is nature's gift. We are called to live, as living companions with nature. Mountains and rivers, the sun and the moon, trees and flowers are all the gifts of God permeating the world with the spirit of God. We have only limited space in Japan, and so when we build a house, we plan it in such a way as to include and integrate the landscape of the background, almost as if it were a part of the backyard. We call it *shakkei*, borrowed view. It widens the horizon of the atmosphere by providing extra natural scenery.

The second important component of atmosphere is people. We are called to live responsibly with our neighbours. To be human means to live among people, sharing one another's joy and suffering. In this sense

Christ manifested full humanity in himself. He shared the atmosphere of suffering. The cross symbolized it, and it is significant that it stood between two other crosses. The cross is not the symbol of a crusade or a conquest as it was often used in later centuries by Western nations. Nor is it for sentimental adornment or decoration. It points to and represents God's determination to be Immanuel, to be God with us, to be God between us, to the extent of sharing our deepest suffering, and thus promises eternal joy and hope to all people. The cross is the symbol of God's togetherness with humanity.

The third dimension of atmosphere is the social organization in which we live. We are living not only in relation to nature and neighbour, but also as part of and relating to nations and countries and amidst the community of nations. Where there is suppression of human rights and the denial of economic justice, the atmosphere of home and community is seriously disturbed. There can be no peace without social justice, no shalom without participation. We are called to make the appropriate response to increase the spirit of justice and work for peace. The salt of the earth, the light of the world and similar biblical expressions define a role rather than bestow a privilege. The role is that of working for peace in a divided world.

Fourthly, we recognize another important dimension in our atmosphere, namely the dimension of time. Not so much in terms of chronological time — when something happened, or how long it took to complete a piece of work, or how many seconds one takes to run a certain distance. A far more important dimension is related to the qualitative meaning of time.

Jesus proclaimed at the beginning of his ministry: "The time is fulfilled and the kingdom of God is at hand; repent, and believe in the gospel" (Mark 1:15). It is the time of fulfilment of all the preparation that had been going on; it is the time of repentance, which is also the time of renewal (*metanoia*), the decisive time to change one's direction.

In this earthly realm the air needs constant "refreshment", as does our human body. Sunday is the time of rest and renewal. I believe one of the unique contributions of the Christian faith is to provide historical hope and renewal, recognizing one's life in between the time of Christ and the final goal of history. This is expressed in a German theological phrase *zwischen den Zeiten* (between the times, meaning the time of Christ and the eschatological time).

So we have four dimensions of our living atmosphere: (1) nature (natural environment), (2) neighbour (personal relationships), (3) nations (social organizations), and (4) newness (historical consciousness and renewal). These four dimensions are just like the four pillars of the household (a living *oikoumene*).

Mandate in nature

The atmosphere is determined by the way we relate ourselves with nature, neighbour, nations (organizations), and newness (historical *metanoia*). I would call them the four dimensions of human responsibility.

I have come to this formulation of ethics partly through my ha-hah experience, but I have also been influenced and stimulated by three outstanding ethical thinkers. One is Tetsuro Watsuji, who used to teach ethics at Tokyo University. He emphasized the impact of *udo*, the geographical and natural climate upon the formation of a particular way of life and culture. From H. Richard Niebuhr, who was an inspiring teacher at Yale, I learned that there is something going on underneath history and in nature and we must make a fitting response to it.

Later on, I was impressed by the life and thought of Dietrich Bonhoeffer, who elaborated on the idea of *mandate* as the locus of responsibility. In his *Ethics,*

Bonhoeffer described four mandates in which God is calling human beings to make the right response. According to him, all created things are created through Christ, with Christ as their end, and co-exist in Christ. In this sense the world is relative to Christ. Furthermore, this relativeness of the world to Christ assumes concrete form in certain mandates of God in the world. Then he names four such mandates: the church, marriage and the family, culture and government.[5]

While I appreciate Bonhoeffer's formulation of mandates, I think he misses an important dimension, namely, the realm of nature as one of the places from which to make a proper response to the divine calling. Both those who speak from the point of view of ecology and those championing the cause of women are re-emphasizing how important it is for human beings to relate themselves to nature. In Asia we are beginning to restore this much-neglected aspect of human responsibility.

In the Bible there is a significant expression of God's love towards all people. It evokes the symbol of the daily sustenance of people. Jesus said: "I am the living bread which came down from heaven" (John 6:51). He taught us to pray: "Give us this day our daily bread" (Matt. 6:11). Furthermore, Jesus often illustrated the coming of the kingdom by the story of a banquet. To it are invited all people from the East and West. They are invited to share the common meal. And the night before he was betrayed, he took bread, and broke it, and distributed it among the disciples, saying: "This is my body given for you" (1 Cor. 11:24).

We tend to consider wheat, or bread, as the symbol of daily food everywhere. But to many Asian people bread is

---

[5] Dietrich Bonhoeffer, *Ethics*, ed. Eberhard Bethge, New York, Macmillan, 1965, p. 291.

a foreign product. It comes from abroad. We Japanese had never seen this kind of food until the Portuguese missionaries and traders brought it to our country about the middle of the sixteenth century. In fact, we still use the Portuguese term for bread, *pan*, in Japanese. The most popular indigenous food has been, and still is, rice. We like rice.

Professor Tadayo Watanabe of Kyoto University has made an extensive study[6] on how the cultivation of rice came to Japan. It had come, by different routes, as early as the Yayoi period. That was the third century. Through his analysis of the varieties of unhulled rice contained in the baked red clay used in ancient Asian monuments, Prof. Watanabe proved that different kinds of rice were cultivated in Asia from very early times — a large type, a round type, a slender type, paddy water rice, upland rice, and so on. He has also proved that what we call Japonica, the sticky round rice, was already in Thailand and Indochina 2000 years ago.

Asia is so big and so diverse. It is not easy to identify Asia. What we have in common is the habit of eating rice, the ubiquitous bamboo, and the use of broken English as a necessary evil for inter-Asian communication.

We can trace the Silk Road along which silk was transported by horses and camels. We can trace the ceramic route taken by boats. Both were primarily for the rulers and the rich. But we can also trace the rice road, and that was used by common people all over Asia. To be sure there were varieties of rice; what one ate depended on geography and personal preference. Nevertheless, it remains true that rice has been and is our daily food in Asia.

It is quite appropriate for us, therefore, to say "God is rice", rather than "God is bread". Kim Chi Ha, the well-

---

[6] *The Rice Road*, 1977.

known Korean Christian poet, who was sent to prison several times in the last ten years, has written the following poem:

> Heaven is rice
> As we cannot go to heaven alone
> We should share rice with one another
> As all share the light of the heavenly stars
> We should share and eat rice together
> Heaven is rice
> When we eat and swallow rice
> Heaven dwells in our body
> Rice is heaven
> Yes, rice is the matter
> We should eat together

The Chinese character for peace, wa, *consists of the radical* 禾 *which pertains to grain, and* 口 *which means mouths. Peace, therefore, is the even distribution of grain or sustenance among the people, or justice.*

It certainly reminds us of the holy communion, which is the occasion to share our daily food together with all people as the symbol of eternal life. This has a social implication as well as a spiritual meaning. The Chinese character for peace (*wa*) literally means harmony. It derives from two words: one is rice and the other is mouth. It means that unless we share rice together with all people, we will not have peace. When every mouth in the whole inhabited world is filled with daily food, then we can have peace on earth.

I would like to analyze some dimensions of the cultivation of rice, primarily from the Japanese context.

Ohayo-culture

To raise rice requires hard and disciplined work. One of our most popular TV programmes in recent years was called *Oshin*, the name of a young girl in the northern part of Japan. Oshin's way of life was marked by hard work, patience and frugality. Max Weber regarded Puritanism as the ethical force which lay behind the spirit of capitalism. The Japanese developed the ethics of hard work and diligence without the Puritan stimulus. This was due partly to the influence of Confucian ethics and partly to natural circumstances.

When we Japanese people meet one another in the morning, we say, *ohayo*, good morning. The literal meaning of *ohayo* is early in the morning. Unlike the nomadic people, who move from one place to another looking for a better location for their cattle, agricultural people normally stay in the same place for a long time. They have to live together in a village harmoniously with nature. Therefore, nature becomes the driving force. The important issue is how harmoniously people live with nature. Do they fight against nature or live in harmony with it?

Yasunari Kawabata, when he received the Nobel Prize in 1968, quoted an old Japanese poem by Dogen (1200-1253):

> In spring the cherry, in summer the cuckoo,
> In autumn the moon, in winter the snow, clear cold.

When I said once that we have four distinct seasons in Japan, an Indian friend remarked: "We also have four seasons. We have a warm season, a hot season, a hotter season, and the hottest season." In Japan the seasons are of utmost importance. Every aspect of Japanese society and culture is determined by the special gift of nature in each of the four seasons. Both the academic year and the fiscal year begin in the spring with the cherry blossoms. Classical forms of poetry, such as *haiku* (17 syllables) and *waka* (31 syllables) are full of references to seasons. The traditional arts of the tea ceremony, flower arrangement, and Japanese cooking are related to the seasons, and contain many symbolic references to seasonal changes.

We know that spring is not too far away when we see the bursting buds on the plum tree. Joseph Hardy Neesima (1843-1890), who founded Doshisha University, expressed his ha-hah experience in these words:

> Truth is just like the winter plum blossom
> It dares to bloom despite snow and wind.

After he returned from his study in the United States, he had this vision of establishing a Christian university in the old capital city of Kyoto. It was a difficult project, impossible according to many of his friends. "To establish a Christian university in a conservative, traditional city is just like commanding Mt Hiei to jump into Lake Biwa," they said. It was the time of the year when the trees had shed all their leaves. But he saw a bud on the branch of a plum tree. It was a foretaste of spring. But it was also the feeling that something was going on here and now, the awakening acknowledgment of "ha-hah!"

We find a similar ha-hah experience in the book of Jeremiah. He was called to be a prophet to the nations. He could not cope with it. "I am only a youth," he said. Then, the word of the Lord came to him saying: "Jeremiah, what do you see?" He said: "I see a rod of almond" (Jer. 1:11). The Hebrew word for almond has also the meaning "to awake". The almond blooms from the end of January to early February, a symbolic sign of the coming spring. At a deeper level it stands for the awakening of people to the living reality of God's presence.

Jesus illustrated the power of the Messianic kingdom by pointing to the way a seed germinates and grows. He said: "The earth produces of itself, first the blade, then the ear, then the grain in the ear" (Mark 4:28). He had observed the potential power which the earth had to bring forth the unfolding process of life from the seed through the blade to the grain. Is it not also a parable of the work of Christ in the whole cosmos?

Let me raise a few points for our consideration.

1. When we say that God is rice we do not mean we should worship rice. We take rice as the symbol of God's gift of life. The statement does not in any way undermine our understanding of God. We stand by our radical monotheism. This point should be emphasized, since there is a strong tendency among the Japanese to take a polytheistic position.

When we think of nature in Japan, we primarily think of the bending bamboo and the tiny chrysanthemums, soft mountains and running streams, not so much of the wild animals in tropical jungles and the African desert. Nature, in our case, is mild and tender. It is full of island moisture permeating a delicate and mysterious atmosphere. People have been trained for thousands of years to live peacefully with nature rather than conquer nature. For us nature is a friend and companion. This is a very important attitude which we should cherish and maintain. But we should resist the temptation to deify nature, to take a particular aspect of nature as an object of worship: that would be polytheism.

2. Second, if we acknowledge that God is rice, the symbolic source of the whole of creation, and if we accept nature as our companion, rather than an object to be conquered or exploited, there will then be a decisive

change in our attitude towards the ecological issue. Obviously then we should strengthen our harmonious relationship with nature and accept responsibility for stewardship. We should "till and keep" the garden with a deep sense of responsibility (Gen. 2:15).

But that is not enough. After all, pollution is still a pressing issue in Japan. Not only pollution at home, but the pollution that is exported. The Japanese, who maintain harmonious relations with nature in their private life, export pollution in various ways to the countries of South-east Asia.

Perhaps we must analyze the social dimension of the rice-raising community, namely, the *furusato*. The term means old home village where people have lived for a long time. (*Furu* means old, and *sato* means village.) As a group of people engaged in rice cultivation, they have lived for a long time in the same place, maintaining a harmonious relationship with nature and with people. This place, both the natural geographical surrounding and the social network of people, we call the *furusato*.

Many Japanese family names are the expression of one's *furusato*, the old village. My name is Takenaka which means bamboo centre. My wife's maiden name is Hayashi which means wood; my sister married a man called Tanaka which means the centre of the rice field. We have many family names which include Ta — rice field, Yamada — mountain rice field, Uchida — inner rice field, Yoshida — blessed rice field, Honda — original rice field, Matsuda — rice field under pine tree, and Toyota — rich rice field. We do not have many Smiths, Bakers or Kissingers in Japan.

Till about a hundred years ago, the majority of Japanese people lived in rural villages. They were engaged in the cultivation of rice. But today only 12 percent of the population is employed in agricultural work. Yet this *furusato* mentality has persisted. It is very much discernible among the contemporary Japanese. In the *furusato* where they had lived for a long time, they knew each other and they helped one another. It was a homogeneous community maintaining a strong sense of belongingness. People had a strong loyalty to the group to which they belonged.

This has influenced the labour-management relations in Japan. At Honda or at Toyota, which are the new *furusato*, both labour and management try to cooperate as partners of the same *furusato* to which they belong.

This means, despite the different interests people have within the group, they demonstrate a tremendous sense of cooperation in the *furusato*, even in the new *furusato*. There is a certain coherent order. Chie Nakane called it *Tate Shakai: a Vertical Society*.[7] Ethical values like loyalty to the group, a seniority system, life-long employment, gradual reform rather than sudden disruption — these are all deeply cherished.

There is, however, a serious drawback in the *furusato* mentality. It is closed on itself, and draws its own boundary lines. One keeps to the group to which one belongs. That is one of the reasons why pollution is still a serious problem, despite the harmonious attitude people have towards nature. The whole nation is in one sense a holy *furusato*. We not only have a sense of belonging to it, we belong only to our nation. It is an absolute commitment. Pollution results out of the cracks in our loyalties, and we export it because our loyalty does not extend beyond our nation.

One of the tasks of Christians in Japan is precisely in this area. While we appreciate the spirit of harmony and loyalty which we have in our Japanese society, we know that we must go beyond the narrow and limited perspective

---

[7] *Japanese Society*, Berkeley, CA, University of California Press, 1970.

of community. We must widen the horizon of *furusato*, beyond our village, our company and even our country. We must widen it in such a way that it embraces the whole earth, the *oikoumene*, the total inhabited world. We must include in it the whole emerging world community.

As the human community, we all face the nuclear threat and the possibility of total annihilation. One of the urgent challenges we face as human beings is to relativize our parochial and national loyalties. As followers of Jesus Christ this is part of our faith commitment. We must indeed redefine our understanding of *furusato*.

3. We live in harmony with nature. Our concept of *furusato* has both positive and negative elements in it. My last point has to do with the question of hope and renewal in the light of "God is rice".

The traditional Japanese image of time is a running stream. Time is a movement of constant change, *mujo*. At a time of parting we exchange cups of rice wine (sake) saying *sayonara*, which means good-bye. What is the literal meaning of *sayonara*?

It is quite natural at the time of taking leave of a friend to express one's good wishes. Good-bye, God be with you, or in the German *Auf-Wiedersehn*, see you again, which is exactly the same as *Zeichen* in Chinese. But the Japanese expression *sayonara* is different; it means "if it is so, let it be so". It reflects an attitude of acceptance, accepting the separation as a matter of course. "We have tried to ponder over the meaning in this separation; but if this is the course of history, let it be so." It takes history as a running stream, whose course we cannot change.

There is a sort of self-negation involved in this *sayonara* attitude. The words Jesus spoke in the garden of Gethsemane, "Not my will but thy will be done" (Matt. 26:42), involve an attitude of self-negation. He accepts humbly what God wants him to do. Jesus had already taught his followers: "…unless a grain of wheat falls into the earth and dies, it remains alone; but if it dies, it bears much fruit" (John 12:24). Here we have the mystery of life and death, or death and life. It prefigured the events of the cross and the resurrection. This attitude of *sayonara* has thus a positive significance since it says good-bye to the old way of life and accepts the new way of life by negating the self.

On the other hand, the *sayonara* mentality can also be dangerous. Because it tends to promote an attitude of resignation, an attitude of passive acceptance of life as it is. It prevents us from engaging in the continuous struggle to bring about historical change. Ironically, Yasunari Kawabata, after attaining high honours, including the Nobel Prize for Literature, the Order of Cultural Merit (the highest cultural award in Japan), and after winning recognition as an outstanding leader in the literary world in Japan and abroad, committed suicide.

Suicide, in fact, is one of the central themes of modern Japanese literature. It is dealt with in the works of Soseki Natsume, Tokoku Kitamura, Takeo Arishima, Ryunosuke Akutagawa, and Osamu Dazai, for example. It is significant that all of them except Soseki committed suicide. But in his famous novel *Kokoro* (*The heart*) the central figure kills himself.

Here, I believe, is the significance of a writer like Rinzo Shiina (1911-1973), who went through a similar period of existential despair but regained an outlook of hope and humour through his encounter with the power of the risen Christ in the Bible.

The image of the fruits

One of the images the early Christians used was the image of the first-fruits.

The time of harvest is drawing near. The first-fruits are in a small bundle that the farmer holds in his hands. They have just been harvested. Christians in Asia Minor, let us remember, were themselves a tiny minority. They lived among the vast majority of people of other faiths which were increasingly becoming secularized.

The Christian minority was called "a kind of first-fruits" (James 1:18). The members of the household of Stephanas were the first-fruits in Achaia (1 Cor. 16:15).

That means they were the first converts in the locality. But this particular, local, small minority — this Christian community — is lifted up in this image as a promise of universal significance. Because of the fact that Christ is the first-fruit — "the first-fruit of those who have fallen asleep" (1 Cor. 15:20). He is a single person, the despised member of a minority, yet he represents the universal victory over death.

The first-fruits are the promise of the Holy Spirit, to whom belongs the greatest harvest to come. In this sense, this image of the first-fruits must give us Asian Christians liberating joy and hope despite our being a small minority. We regain our hope when we remember Christ's promise: "Fear not, little flock, for it is your Father's good pleasure to give you the kingdom" (Luke 12:32).

I have tried to describe three characteristics of the Japanese way of life: the harmonious relationship with nature, people's participation and togetherness in the *furusato* community, and the attitude of *sayonara*. I have tried to describe them not only through the method of ha-hah discernment but also through a dialectical way of seeing critically both their positive and negative aspects and of looking for their point of transformation in the light of the Christian faith.

I would now like to proceed to examine the question of Christ and culture in the Asian setting.

2. Christ and Culture in Asia

Culture and cult

Literally the word "culture" means cultivation, or the state of being cultivated. "Cult" means religious worship and ritual. There is a close affinity between the different kinds of work we do in relation to nature: *agriculture* and *cult*, religious ritual and *culture*, the various artistic expressions of people.

As an example of a cultural expression in relation to the appreciation of nature in a time of suffering, I would like to introduce a couple of poems, written by Ikuko Uchida, a Japanese-American woman who died in 1966. She went over to California in 1917 at the age of 24 to marry Takashi Uchida. They had been introduced to each other by their teacher at Doshisha. She and her husband were devoted members of the Sycamore Congregational Church in Oakland, where they lived with their two daughters. They had made California their new *furusato*. Ikuko was of great help to many Japanese people who came to the United States for higher studies. I was one of them. She was rather a reserved person, yet very sensitive to the needs of others. Wherever she was, she quietly created a warm atmosphere with her hospitality and motherly care. Some of her poems, through which she expressed her sense of joy and sorrow, still touch our inner heart. In seeing the budding plum, she writes:

> The budding plum
> Holds my own joy
> At the melting of ice
> And the long winter's end

Seeing a little flower on a quiet rainy day she is reminded of the sound of *koto* (a traditional Japanese string instrument):

> Like the sound of a *koto* on a quiet rainy day
> So, too, this small flower brings comfort to my heart

During the time of the Second World War, the family was forced to go to an "evacuation camp". First her husband was interned in the army camp in Missoula, Montana. One of the daughters, now a distinguished writer, described the time of separation:

When it was time to say goodbye, none of us could speak for the ache in our heart. My sister and I began to cry. And it was Mama who was the strong one.[1]

Then in the following year, 1942, the other members of the family were also sent to a camp, first at Tanforan and later at Topaz, a desert city in Utah. Here there were no flowers, not even any grass. All they could see was the blue sky. In the evening, the moon rose behind the dark mountains.

Someone named it Topaz ... This land
Where neither grass nor trees
Nor wild flowers grow.
The camp was cruelly crowded. There was no privacy. It was very depressing.

Grown old so soon. In a foreign land,
What do they think, these people,
Eating in lonely silence?

It is not my purpose to criticize Executive Order 9066, which was issued on 19 February 1942 by President Roosevelt. It caused much hardship and pain, but it also led to many acts of kindness and love. In the midst of the mounting tension and prejudice, many citizens of the United States, individually and institutionally, provided immediate and practical help to meet the needs of people caught up in a panic situation. My purpose is only to point out how the art form of *waka* and Christian faith came together concretely in the person of Ikuko Uchida, a Japanese-American woman, and how it sustained her in a situation of existential anguish, and how it has continued to sustain others in similar situations.

The Creator's blessings overflow
And even the single lily has its soul[2]

[1] Yoshiko Uchida, *Desert Exile*, p.48.
[2] The original *waka* by Ikuko Uchida, English translation by Yoshiko Uchida, in *Desert Exile*, p.145.

A listening approach to visual art

Obviously seeing is a very important part of knowing and loving. We have to stop and see the reality in order to understand and appreciate what is going on. But the traditional Oriental painting stresses the importance of listening in visual art. Certainly life in the atmosphere, in nature, in a sanctuary, or in a tea house, is mobile and liquid. It has colour and shape which we see. But if we "see" only what we have seen, then we would be aware only of the external technique and the surface reality.

The Oriental approach to art emphasizes the art of listening, even in the case of visual art. This may appear strange. Is not visual art "visual"? In it normally we stress the colour and the form of the object. Music, of course, is different; in it we emphasize sound and rhythm. But this is a false division of labour. Beiu Iizuka, one of the leaders of the black and white Oriental painting, *nanga*, remarked:

> While Western painting stresses colour and shape, Eastern painting emphasizes the voice. When we see the waterfall we listen to the sound of the waterfall. When we see the birds we listen to the singing of the birds. When we see a flower we listen to the song of the flower.

The heart of a painting is to express the sound of the waterfall, the singing of birds, and the song of the flower. This is the reason why in *nanga* they usually use black Chinese ink, called *sumi*, on white paper. A simple black and white medium will express the sound of life and spirit much better than more elaborate media.

Talking about the kingdom of God, Jesus said: "The wind blows where it wills, and you hear the sound of it" (John 3:8). The sound of wind does not have colour or shape and cannot be painted by a rational technique. It must be grasped by the heart which throbs to the echo it brings. It is the ha-hah approach in art.

This word echo, *hibiki*, 響 in Chinese characters, consists of two parts, *sound* and *furusato*, old village. "God created man and woman in his own image" (Gen. 1:27). Does not that suggest that we need the capacity of "imaging" in response to God's message in the cosmos? The power of imagination is of the utmost importance; it is the ability to respond to the echo of life.

The renewal of the Chinese Christian community

One of the central issues in Christian art in Asia is that of interpreting Christ through our Asian mind and of expressing the image of Christ through Asian culture. Recently I visited the church in China as a member of a delegation of the National Christian Council of Japan. I was amazed to see the new vitality of the Christian community in China. At one of the Sunday services we attended in Shanghai there were some 3,000 worshippers. Even more than the size of the congregation, the atmosphere of the church service impressed me. They sang many new hymns expressing the joy of faith and hope. One could not help thinking of their recent experience of suffering. In Nanjing Union Seminary, where about 190 students are studying, they offer two courses on Christian art, one an introductory course and the other a more advanced course for those who want to specialize in the area of Chinese Christian art.

Despite the tremendous efforts of Western missionaries and despite the fact that more missionary personnel and funds were sent to China than to most other "fields", very few Chinese were converted to Christianity. At the time of China's liberation in 1949 the number of Protestants in the country was not over 700,000. Today their number has gone up to three million according to a conservative estimate. K.H. Ting points out the reason for the growth of the church:

> People, of course, have become Christians out of many different circumstances, but the one underlying reason

behind all these circumstances is that, today, the church in China has shed much of its Western image. Its Chineseness is not only apparent in the personnel of the leadership and in the source of its financial support, but also in its growth in ways of expressing the Christian faith: its thought, its worship, and its art and music.[3]

In the old days, Ting said, if a Chinese became a Christian, it meant the nation lost one Chinese. At that time the church was dominated by foreign personnel and foreign culture. Christianity was considered a Western religion, and it came wrapped in Western culture.

Now there is a deep commitment on the part of the Chinese Christians to follow Christ as Chinese people and to worship God within the Chinese culture and with Chinese sensitivity. It is the beginning of the significant process of "de-Westernization of Christianity" and the "Chinization of Christianity".

Just as Kanzo Uchimura (1861-1930) could say: "I love two Js: one is Jesus and the other is Japan", so too the Chinese Christians can now say: "We love two C's; one is Christ, and the other is China." And this nationalism is not chauvinistic nationalism. There is plenty of room in it for prophetic criticism. It also allows for self-criticism. It expresses itself in sorrow over the tragedy of the people and the nation, and in joy over the people's liberation and achievements.

Images of Christ in Asia

A couple of years ago, Asian Christian artists met outside Manila, Philippines, in order to try to discern together the responsibility of Christian artists. They met around the theme "The Magnificat Today in Asia". Despite the variety of backgrounds, geographical and cultural, and the political and denominational differences, they shared certain common concerns.

---

[3] *A Rationale for the Three-Self Movement*, Neeshima Lecture, 28 September, 1984.

How can we interpret and express Christ in Asia today? What is our image of Christ as Asian artists? How can this image of Christ be shared with the people of other faiths and ideologies? What is the social role or prophetic task of Christian artists in the midst of the poverty and the oppression which are so widespread in Asia?

We find in the Magnificat not only the exaltation of a humble woman but also God's promise of lifting up the poor and bringing down the mighty from their thrones. The rich must go away with empty hands (Luke 1:52-53).

A flat-nosed Christ

One of the artists at the consultation, Jyoti Sahi from India, told us a story about Sri Ramakrishna (1836-1886) who was for some time a Hindu priest at the Kali temple. Ramakrishna had a vision of Christ which lasted for three days.

> On the fourth day, as he was walking in the Panchavati, there was an extraordinary-looking person of serene aspect approaching him with his gaze intently fixed on him. He knew him at once to be a man of foreign extraction. He had beautiful large eyes, and though the nose was a little flat it in no way marred the comeliness of his face. Sri Ramakrishna was charmed and wondered who he might be. Presently the figure drew near, and from the inmost recesses of Sri Ramakrishna's heart there went up the note: "There is the Christ who poured out his heart's blood for the redemption of mankind and suffered agonies for its sake. It is none else but that Master-Yogi, Jesus, the embodiment of Love!"[4]

It is interesting that, as Christ appeared to him, he had a foreign look, but the nose was flat. This flat-nosed Christ kept coming up again and again in Sri Ramakrishna's life, because the vision had made a deep impression on him. Long after, discussing Christ with his disciples, he asked:

---

[4] *The Life of Sri Ramakrishna*, 6th ed., 1948, p.253f.

"Well, you have read the Bible. Tell me what it says about the features of Christ. What did he look like?" They answered: "We have not seen this particularly mentioned anywhere in the Bible; but Jesus was born among the Jews, so he must have been fair, with large eyes and an aquiline nose." Sri Ramakrishna only remarked: "But I saw his nose was a little flat — who knows why." Not attaching much importance to those words at the time, the disciples, after the passing away of Sri Ramakrishna, heard that there were three extant descriptions of Christ's features, and one of these actually described him as flat-nosed![5]

This is an illuminating story. It speaks of the acknowledgment of the image of Christ by one who is not a Christian. It shows that the power of Christ is not limited within the walls of the church or the limits of the Christian community. C.S. Song comments on this event:

What interests us most in the story is that Christ appeared to Sri Ramakrishna as flat-nosed. We wonder why Christ did not appear to him as a full-fledged Semite, Anglo-Saxon, or Indo-European. "Flat-nosed" being a common description, rightly or wrongly, of people of Asian or, in particular, Mongolian extraction, Christ with a flat nose must have bothered Sri Ramakrishna a great deal. Perhaps this is why he referred to it again later.[6]

A flat nose is a common feature among Asians, especially among the ordinary people in Asia. If God in Jesus Christ is the God Incarnate, the word become flesh, for an Asian it is quite natural to imagine him as the flat-nosed Christ. Furthermore, according to Jyoti Sahi, the flat-nosed Christ in the Indian cultural setting has a spiritual meaning. In many places the flat-nosed tribal people are looked down upon. They are often humiliated.

---

[5] Swami Ghanananda, *Sri Ramakrishna and His Unique Message*, 3rd ed., 1970, pp.91-92, quoted in Richard V. Taylor, *Jesus in Indian Paintings*, The Christian Literature Society, 1975, pp.77-78.
[6] *The Compassionate God*, Maryknoll, NY, Orbis, 1981, p.2.

Christ humbled himself, even to the extent of taking the form of a slave; he not only washed the feet of the disciples, he even gave "his life as a ransom for many" (Mark 10:45).

This too is in accordance with the words of the Magnificat, in which Mary sang: "My soul magnifies the Lord, and my spirit rejoices in God my Saviour. For he has regarded the low estate of his handmaiden" (Luke 1:46-48). We see many examples of the flat-nosed Mary among the works of Asian artists.[7]

A mis-shapen-nosed Christ

One of the most appealing artistic pieces I saw in India was by K.C.S. Paniker. It is called "The Sorrow of Christ" (see next page). Paniker was a noted Indian artist and art teacher. In 1957 he became principal of the Government College of Arts and Crafts in Madras. After his retirement, he helped organize a village of young artists, outside Madras city at a place called Cholamondal. I remember visiting him there. I took a jeep from Madras. It was a hot day, and the road was dusty. It took almost two hours to reach the place. Paniker, white-bearded, welcomed me. He was at that time 62 years old. He took me to his studio and showed me this sculpture called "The Sorrow of Christ". I asked him: "Tell me, what led you to do this work?" He said: "I am a Hindu. We contemplate, and pray and fast. We meditate on the way of compassion. I read the Bible at Madras Christian College where I studied. I was impressed to find that this man, Jesus of Nazareth, not only prayed for, but actually related himself to the misery of marginalized people, such as those who suffered from leprosy."

The sculpture vividly shows the compassion of Christ, identifying with the misery of suffering people. His nose

---

[7] See Masao Takenaka, *Christian Art in Asia*, Tokyo, Kyo Bun Kwan, 1975.

is distorted. His mouth is mis-shapen and his eyes pop out. I thought this Christ, of the mis-shapen nose, is one of the most penetrating images of Christ in Asia where the physical condition of leprosy and the social status of the outcast are still a part of our existential reality.

Embracing Christ
    We have seen that a harmonious attitude towards nature is one of the characteristic ways of life in Asia. To be sure such harmony is not a uniform phenomenon. It arises out of diversity, just as the harmonies of the choir and the orchestra, where each sound has a distinctive identity, and

each instrument makes a unique contribution, are all essential and important. Certainly unity is important, but unity is not conformity; it is unity in diversity and variety in harmony, and it respects the distinctive identity of the participants or constituents.

It is very important to keep this in mind, as we are living in an increasingly technological era, and the impact of universal technology tends to overshadow local cultures, and to obscure rather than promote local identity.

We are indeed entering a new stage of our pilgrimage in human history; we need to take each basic culture seriously in order to attain the unity of humankind. Local and ethnic cultures cannot be given up for the sake of a national or international culture. In our common pilgrimage, the local and ethnic identity should not be an appendage to national life. It goes beyond national boundaries since it touches something essential and basic to human life. It invites echoes and aspirations of the universal.

The spirituals and the blues sung by the black people in the midst of their agony and their search for hope contain a universal appeal. They deal with the local and, precisely because of their particularity, they extend to the universal.[8]

Here we must recognize the very important role of art. It is rooted in local culture, but it can also make a distinctive contribution to the emergence of a world community.

Recognizing the Spirit of Christ which embraces the whole cosmos (Col. 1:15-17; Eph. 4:14-23), we need to point out the following two factors, the artistic expression of the Christ Mandala and the creative power of women in Asian art.

---

[8] James Cone, *The Spirituals and Blues*, New York, The Seabury Press, 1972.

Christ Mandala: Many Asian Christian artists such as Jyoti Sahi, Nalini Jayasuriya, and Alphonso are utilizing the rythmic form of the circle and centre to express the presence of Christ. They clearly and simply place Christ at the centre and in that representation he embraces the cosmos as a whole. Take, for example, the painting of

Christ Mandala by Nalini Jayasuriya. She is a third-generation Christian from Sri Lanka, where Buddhism is the predominant religion. To be sure, there are numerous expressions of mandalas, varying according to locality, such as the Tibetan Mandala, Chinese Mandala, Japanese Mandala. The original meaning of mandala is "assembly".

According to the most ordinary interpretation, mandala means a circle.[9]

In Nalini Jayasuriya's Christ Mandala, we find in the centre the Christ figure. He is seated in the lotus posture of meditation with his hands in a Mandala gesture of blessing. He is surrounded by a circle which can be interpreted as a mandala or halo (a ring of light) representing the glory of God. Or it can be read as a mandala of a circle of light showing Christ as the centre of the universe. To the left and right are four small human figures representing the four evangelists (left above, Matthew, the human figure; left below, Mark, the lion; right below, Luke, the ox; and right above, John, the eagle). We also note that above the figure of Christ there are three red suns representing the Trinity, and all the motifs float on a sea of fine circular lines suggestive of the vibrations that radiate from the centre outwards and back again.

This image of mandala contains a special significance since it overcomes the dualistic notion which prevailed strongly in Western Christianity. The rational and dualistic approach to life puts Christians in a handicapped situation today. Even today, the underlying assumptions involve a dualistic interpretation — separating the spirit from the body, the secular from the sacred, the paternal and the maternal, heaven and earth, positive and negative, and good and evil. Despite the fact that such a dichotomization of life has been challenged and corrected, the basic structure of meaning has not been changed drastically within the Christian community.

Oh Jae Shik, who served as the Christian Conference of Asia's secretary for urban and industrial mission work in Asia in the decade of the seventies, has pointed out the

---

[9] Chikyo Yamamoto, *Introduction to the Mandala*, Kyoto, Doshisha, 1980, p.4.

social implications of the dualistic approach in the following way:

> There is... the latent attitude in the Christian community that the spirit is more valuable than the body, and that the body may be shared for the sake of the spirit. As a corollary, Christians protect their spiritual territory jealously but are less concerned about the destruction of the body. They fight hard to protect the sanctuary but are careless about what is happening in torture chambers. This attitude has profound social implications. (It assumes) that earthly matters can be sacrificed for the sake of heavenly concerns. Hence Christians are more concerned with authority and order in a society, but careless about the destruction of the earth. The groaning of the earth and the cries from the torture chamber have not reached Christian ears.[10]

Women in the birth of life: The Magnificat was sung by a humble woman. She went to the hill country, to the house of Zechariah. As she greeted Elizabeth the babe leaped in her womb (Luke 1:39-41). I see in this a striking example of the ha-hah approach in the Bible. It was recognition and acceptance. In response to the blessing of Elizabeth, Mary sang the song which we know as the Magnificat.

Here, surely, we can have no reservation in recognizing and celebrating the creative and imaginative power given by God to the woman. Mary's song is marked by deep humility, but it is also a powerful statement of faith and hope. It contains tremendous implications for our social relationships.

But we have had other Magnificats. At times of oppression and apparent hopelessness, many Asian mothers have sung songs which remind us of Mary's song. Here is the prayer of a Korean mother when her two sons were arrested in the spring of 1974, together with

---

[10] "Social Movement and the Role of Symbols", address at the Second Consultation of Christian Art in Asia, March 1984.

hundreds of Korean students who were protesting the repressive actions of the government:

> O Father God, since our beloved sons have been in prison, spring has passed and summer has changed into chilly fall, and in a few days we will be celebrating *chusok* (the harvest moon festival).

The mother prayed not only for the liberation of her children, she also prayed for others as well, with a sense of repentance. She prayed for forgiveness and the gift of neighbourliness.

> We could not really understand the suffering of Christ's Cross; forgive us the sin of being concerned only that our own children have success in life. Forgive us that although we saw the plight of many poverty-stricken neighbours, we did not put forth the effort to be true neighbours to them.[11]

This woman is humble and strong at the same time. In the realm of art, we often recognize the creative power in response to the rhythm of life. Women are blessed with the ability to conceive and give birth to life, which is precisely the central concern of art. One of the young Korean women artists speaks:

> By their very nature women are artistic, for they know the rhythm of life in its power and its mysterious depth. Women have an inherent power to endure suffering. Endurance is the capacity to participate in the agony of life and to overcome a deviant state of life, leading it into new creation. This is not passivity, but the will for creation and the ceaseless desire for life. Women, being privileged to partake in the rhythm of life, can witness to the mysterious power of life. The act of witnessing to life is integrative, not divisive; comprehensive, not partial; and creative, not destructive.[12]

---

[11] *Documents on the Struggle for Democracy in Korea*, Tokyo, Shinkyo Shuppansha, 1975, pp.205-206.
[12] Kim Jae-Im, "Women and Art", *Image*, No. 21, September 1984.

This power given to women to conceive and to create is very much related to the gift of God in nature. We can thus understand why *ikebana*, the art of flower arrangement, is popular among Japanese women. In *ikebana* we learn from nature how flowers grow in the field, and change with the seasons. *Ikebana* is not merely an imitation of nature. It is an art which expresses the philosophy of life through the flower. One of its great exponents in the eighteenth century was Mishosai Ippo who formulated the triangular style of *ikebana* to express the cosmic harmony between heaven, earth, and human beings.

A flower is not only tiny, it is also fragile. It represents a passing form of earthly existence. It withers in no time, and that is one reason why we cherish it. It is something to be loved before it dies. We see the mortality of our lives in the falling flower petals.

Kyoko Grant, who has served the Asian Christian Art Association as the editor of *Image*, is an *ikebana* teacher. As a Christian woman, she gives a religious interpretation of *ikebana*:

> We try to see an eternal quality in the transitory nature of our lives. In this we can glimpse the boundary between life and death. We don't see merely with our eyes, but we sense it with our inner vision. *Ikebana* spiritualizes the flower.[13]

We call to mind how Christ reminded us of the sustaining grace of God by saying: "If God so clothes the grass of the field, which today is alive and tomorrow is thrown into the oven, will he not much more clothe you?" (Matt. 6:30). Here again the stress is not only on its beauty in simplicity, but also on its mortality, symbolically pointing to the abiding love of God in the boundary between life and death. Therefore, we want to live today with hope, and not be overly anxious about tomorrow.

---

[13] *Image*, No. 19, March 1984.

Here is a song Fred Kaan and I once composed when we were in Indonesia. We were reflecting on the life of a nameless flower, in relation to human rights in Asia.

> We who bear the human name are like flowers of the field;
> Without status, without fame, trampled down and made to yield,
> Unprotected and exposed to the scorching wind that blows.
> Let all the world now blossom as a field!
>
> Even Solomon of old, said our Lord the man of peace,
> With his glory and his gold could not match the flower's grace.
> We are weak, but we recall how the mighty men must fall.
> Let all the world now blossom as a field.
>
> We are people of the field, crowding Asia's city streets.
> We are people called to build a community of peace
> We remember as we toil hope is springing from the soil.
> Let all the world now blossom as a field.[14]

The prophetic task of art

There are people who consider a work of art as a luxury, because its enjoyment can be time-consuming and expensive. Asian Christians are not rich. They are, the majority of them, from humble backgrounds. It is understandable if they consider works of art as an extra and as belonging to the domain of the affluent. Nevertheless, I would like to emphasize the prophetic dimension of art. It can inspire people to struggle for justice and peace. A nude figure by Picasso is an example of a very expensive — and luxurious — kind of art, while his *Guernica*, as Paul Tillich pointed out, contains a prophetic message. It depicts a scene of utter horror — everything broken to pieces because of indiscriminate bombing.

---

[14] *Cantate Domino*, Oxford University Press, 1980, pp.247-248.

In Japan some time ago we had a touring exhibition of art works on Hiroshima by Iri and Toshi Maruki who jointly produced pieces portraying the horror of destruction. Young people committed to peace and an anti-nuclear stance sponsored the exhibition.[15] The supporters of the exhibition were not rich people, but each of them contributed a small sum towards this mobile exhibition throughout Japan. It had a considerable impact.

It is expensive to buy works of art. And few of us can afford to be collectors. That is why we should strengthen efforts to make art the common property of the community rather than an individual's private acquisition.

Moreover, in recent years we have come to recognize increasingly the creative capacity of people who were long suppressed by national and technocratic powers. This can become an international force. Local people are often not only divided but also victimized by the larger system. Sometimes people become too tense and internal divisions develop among them; at other times, an atmosphere of fear and conformity sets in, and people lose all interests except those of sheer survival. But even in such an atmosphere we can discern an invisible wind blowing among the people.

In Japan we now have the Folk Art (*Mingei*) Movement, as a result of the rediscovery of the simple, local art of the people. It is made up of the work of ordinary people. Through their humble, often reproduced and simple work, they have created extraordinarily beautiful pieces, not for exhibition in the museum, but for ordinary, daily use.

People in the islands of Okinawa are known for their folk art, both in music and pottery. In the feudalistic period, Okinawa was suppressed by the war lords, either

---

15 *The Joint Works of Iri Maruki and Toshi Maruki*, Maruki Gallery for Hiroshima Panel Foundation, 1983.

of southern China or of Japan. During the Second World War, the islands became bloody battle fields. It was for the people of the islands a time of sorrow and deprivation. The people of the Okinawa islands have also suffered the ravages of typhoons almost every year. The folk songs and dances in Okinawa reflect something of the spirit of sorrow and desolation which the people have experienced through centuries. Through crafts, poems, stories, music, and dance they express their inner anguish and unarticulated hope, not only to communicate with one another, but also to form a reservoir of common memory and aspiration.

Today similarly we are rediscovering the meaning of the mask dance among the suppressed people (minjung) in Korea. The mask dance expresses their long-accumulated suffering, *han*, and it serves a conscientizing role. The common people are encouraged to take steps towards their own liberation. Here symbols play an important role, opening up the level of reality which exists but remains hidden and unrecognized. The task of the prophet is not so much to present us with a new reality as to reveal what remains hidden and disclose its ambiguity and its promise for the future. The prophet opens up the hearts and souls of people, directing their attention to something new to come in the future.

In the Philippines, in response to the cry of the people, especially after the assassination of Senator Aquino, a few artists formed a group called Concerned Artists of the Philippines. They wanted to express in their work their concern over the oppression and exploitation of people. They wanted to fight the structures of injustice in their own country as well as in other third-world nations. One of the leading artists in the group, Edgar Fernandez, has portrayed Mary as a Philippine young mother standing with the poor and oppressed. He expressed his conviction in the following way:

I felt that I had to portray this (the parallels of the life of Mary and her son Jesus with that of the Philippine people) in my paintings and in my everyday life as a Christian: to give life to Christ's teachings; to liberate the consciousness of the oppressed; and to inspire others to help the poor and those who are not yet enlightened.[16]

To describe the Magnificat in the painting, he used the old alphabet, *alibeta*, as a part of the design because he thought that Asian art combined both poetry and painting. Here again listening and seeing go together in Asian art.

The church: the community of the Magnificat

We have been discussing the image of Christ, and how it may be mediated through art and incarnated in culture. But what should be the image of the church?

We know we are going through a time of great changes. But we are not sure what the changes are and where they are leading us. It is like the time of the Magnificat — the time of "birthing". Mary was sure that something new was coming, but she was not sure of the exact form and shape of the One that was coming. In fact she is constantly on the road: going to see Elizabeth, going to Bethlehem, going to Egypt, and later searching for her son in the temple, going to Jerusalem, even going to Golgotha. In our time of radical change, "the time of birthing", what is coming is the new world community. In order to help with its coming, we too should be "on the road" trying to discern together the signs of the times and the signposts on the way. One of the important requisites, as we face the future, is the attitude of openness.

The professional church leader would say, since Mary found Jesus in the church, you'd better come to the church. Theoretically, that is certainly right. But a more

---

[16] *Image*, No.20, July 1984.

important theological question is, which kind of church? I do not mean to introduce a complex and much-discussed ecclesiological problem. But in the light of "the birthing", and the renewing experience of Christian art in Asia, we may want to ask: What are the emerging forms of the Christian community?

The more we study the cultural roots of Asia, despite the different patterns, the more we recognize one common factor. It is that both religion and culture are closely related to community. As Tagore rightly pointed out, joy, *ananda*, arises from communion or sharing. Under the auspices of the traditional cultures, Asian religions hold joyful festivals and community celebrations, not inside the temple or shrine, but outside in the open spaces in the community. I believe this is biblical.

> Behold, how good and pleasant it is when brothers (and sisters) dwell in unity (together, in communion)! It is like the dew of Hermon, which falls on the mountains of Zion (Ps. 133).

Charles Correa, a contemporary creative architect in India, was asked: How do you think Indian church buildings should reflect Indian cultural values? He pointed out:

> The building expresses an attitude towards space. All Western architecture goes back to the Vitruvian box. Vitruvius was a Roman architect and engineer who wrote a detailed theoretical work on the principles of architecture in the first century before Christ. For him, essentially, the rhythms of architectural form were contained within the walls of the building.
> Most traditional Western church architecture is essentially a space within a box. But in the East, space has been thought of as limitless. You approach the temple through space. The journey to the temple stresses the sense of space. The area around the temple and the path that goes round the temple

precincts define the space of the temple. Space is outside the temple, not inside it.[17]

There is a renewed interest in church buildings in Asia. The present church building is one of the colonial inheritances of the Asian church. It has the Western box-church form. It is an enclosed shell. In the tropical climate it is too hot inside. Moreover, spiritually it tends to be cut off from the rest of the community like the meeting room of a Western secret society.

Jyoti Sahi remarked: "We forget that much of our ecclesiology is based on Roman or Greek mystery religions where baptism was all-important as an entry point to the cult; this kind of ecclesiology leads ultimately to the closed box church."[18]

What we need today is an open church, a pilgrim church, a celebrating church, where the people of God do not want to close themselves in, or close themselves off, but are willing to be with the people in the community — even as Christ shared his life with all people.

Here the movement takes a reverse direction — rather than from baptism to communion, it moves from communion to baptism, from the work of bringing justice and peace in the world to witnessing in the community, from the common sharing of joy and suffering with the people in community to the occasion of dedication in the sanctuary. We seek to be the church of the Magnificat, the church rejoicing in the "birthing" of Jesus into the human community.

---

[17] *Image*, No. 21, September 1984.

[18] *Ibid*.

3. The Ethics of Betweenness

A case study of Shozo Tanaka (1841-1913)

There are four reasons why I want to consider the life and thought of Shozo Tanaka.

First, he was one of the pioneers of the people's movement in modern Japan. He was a peasant. Until the end of his life he remained in a rural area and worked for the welfare of the land and the people in the rural community. Although he went to Tokyo several times as a member of the national Diet, his main concern continued to be the protection of the rights of people in the local village. I believe that we need to keep in mind the examples of men and women who have made quiet contributions through their struggles to protect and enhance human life and the conditions of the natural environment, especially in rural areas and local provinces where the majority of Asian people still live, often in dehumanizing conditions. In this age of mass communication we remember those who made names in the big cities but tend to forget those who made lasting contributions through their persistent struggles in rural areas. In a long-range perspective, sometimes it is not easy to determine who are the minor and who the major prophets!

The second reason I take up the life of Shozo Tanaka is the availability of original materials which were discovered recently, and the fact that the *Complete Works of Shozo Tanaka* have now been published. It took four years to complete the publication of all nineteen volumes. They contain the autobiography (Vol.I), the articles (Vol.I-Vol.V), the speeches and records of the national Diet and prefectural legislature (Vol.VI-Vol.VIII), the diary (Vol.IX-Vol.XIII), and the letters (Vol.XIV-Vol.XIX).[1] It is amazing that he wrote so extensively both in his private and public life. To be sure, Shozo Tanaka

---

[1] 1972; all quotations from these volumes.

was not entirely unknown before the publication of *The Complete Works*. Several fragmentary writings were available concerning his life. But now we have most of his original writings, which makes it possible to trace his life historically and to analyze his thoughts as a whole systematically. One of the difficulties of the so-called "local people's history" is the lack of original documents. Many of our farmers do not write much; they leave no records. Therefore it is not easy to trace their historical path and to study their thinking. But in the case of Shozo Tanaka we have enough original materials to reconstruct his life and to study his ethical ideas.

Thirdly, I am interested in Tanaka since he has been consistently dealing with the question of land. One can say he was almost a single-issue strategist. Yet, as he dug deeper into the issue, he came to see the inter-relationship of land (nature), people (neighbours), state (nation), and history (newness). For example, as he studied in greater depth aspects of the copper mine issue (on the use of land), he recognized the inter-relationship between personal ethics and social ethics, between morality and religion, and the wellbeing of nature and the health of humanity.

Fourthly, I am interested in Shozo Tanaka's case because he was committed to the Christian faith. He was not an ardent member of the institutional church. He was not educated in a mission school nor did he receive special support from a missionary. His teacher was Osui Arai, who introduced him to Christianity, though he met Arai only occasionally. His main contact with Christianity was through the Bible, which he read for the first time in prison in 1902; after that he read it again and again all by himself.

He used to carry a portion of the Bible (the Gospel according to Matthew) and the Japanese constitution in his kimono. I like to think of what kind of biblical texts most appealed to him, and how he related the biblical message to the teachings of other Japanese religions, including Buddhism and Confucianism.

More specifically, what was the ethical approach of Shozo Tanaka, and what leasons can we learn from his life as we think of Christian obedience in an Asian context?

Who was Shozo Tanaka?

Shozo Tanaka was born on 3 November 1841, in the village of Nakamura, Shimotsuke, now Tochigi prefecture, about 150 kilometres north of Tokyo. He writes in his autobiography: "I am a peasant of Shimotsuke"; and he grew up a peasant and the son of peasants in that rural village.

His father's name was Tomizo and his mother's Saki. Both were respected members of the community. Like his grandfather, his father was elected *nanushi*, the village master. In 1859, when Shozo was eighteen years old, he was elected village master, soon after his father was promoted to the position of *warimoto*, the leader whose job is to coordinate the affairs of the six villages of the region.

He has described in his writings episodes from his boyhood which tell us something of his character. He was a stubborn boy. On a rainy night, when he was five years old, he painted the face of a doll and showed it to a servant who was apparently not very impressed. Shozo was angry; he put the brush and ink in front of the servant, and asked him to paint it better. The servant apologized, but Shozo went on insisting that he should paint the doll. His mother, who happened to overhear the conversation, asked him to stop pestering the servant. But he was adamant. The mother, in shame, went out into the night and stood quietly in the rain for two hours. Recollecting this event, Shozo said:

> This punishment left a deep mark on my heart and caused a genuine sense of repentance. I believe it was the harsh

discipline of my mother which helped me to change my attitude towards the people working for me.

One day when he made a business visit to a neighbouring village, he was asked to deliver a message to a weaver there. He finished his work but completely forgot to give the message. Upon his return, when his neighbour came to collect the reply he dashed back to the village, a considerable distance, and delivered the message to the weaver. The message was a brief one: "Please finish my piece as quickly as possible." The story indicates his deep sense of responsibility.

Indeed, throughout his life he was a man of integrity; he made an effort to keep every promise he made to the people. When he was a boy, he devoted himself to agricultural work very diligently from early morning. Since the income he got through normal agricultural work was so small, he also took to the cultivation of indigo.

Shozo was not an eloquent speaker. In fact, he was an awkward one. Also he did not have a strong memory. This is rather surprising, since later on he became a political leader and used to make long speeches quoting detailed statistics in relation to the effects of pollution.

He was committed to the cause of people, and worked for justice on their behalf. In 1868, Shozo openly accused a leading elder of corrupt practices, and he was arrested and sent to prison. He was confined to a small cell for ten months and twenty days.

Shozo did not have much education or legal knowledge, but he had an untiring spirit and he was a persistent fighter for justice. He said:

As a person who holds a public office, if I accept a responsibility I will continue to struggle to actualize my calling in spite of the stormy wind and the heavy rain. Even if it involves the sacrifice of my work and property, I will not give up until we reach the goal.

He went to prison for the second time when he was thirty years old. By then he was an officer of Esashi (now Aomori) Prefecture, and he was falsely charged with the assassination of his superior. He was in prison for three years and twenty days, 1871-1874. During this period he read for the first time translations of some Western writings on human rights. In order to improve his ability to speak, he read aloud the Japanese translation of Samuel Smile's *Self-help*.

In 1878, when he was thirty-seven, Shozo decided to dedicate the rest of his life to a political calling. Because of high inflation just after the Seinan war, the value of his land had increased more than ten times. He decided to sell the land and use the money for public causes through his political involvement. He drew up a financial plan to maintain himself in political life for the next thirty-five years and discussed the matter with his father.

> Shozo has 40,000,000 brothers and sisters. Half are parents and elders and the other half are younger brothers and sisters. The heaven is the roof of our house and the earth is the floor.

His father was very happy to hear of his son's decision. He encouraged him with these words:

> It is no use to become a *Hotoke* (Buddhist saint) after one's death. The important thing is to become a good man while living in this world.

Shozo was elected to the local legislature in 1880 and worked for the civil liberties movement, especially advocating the election of the national Diet by popular vote. In 1884 he was imprisoned for a third time because of his opposition to Governor Mishima of Tochigi Prefecture. In 1890, in the first election for the national Diet, Shozo was elected a member of the Lower House (analogous to the House of Representatives). He was a member until 1901, when he resigned.

He made his first public speech during the debate over the pollution from the Ashio copper mine, near Yanaka village, at the second session of the Diet in 1891. The mine owner — with the support of the central government — made an attempt to settle the issue by negotiating privately with some of the victims, thus trying to isolate those peasants who protested. There were several violent incidents. Tanaka consistently advocated non-violent resistance. In 1898, as the accumulated anger of the peasants came to a head, a violent confrontation seemed imminent. Then Shozo made this promise to the group of peasants who were on the road to Tokyo for a massive demonstration:

> I am a member of the Diet who knows of this pollution case and the situation of the victims. Therefore, I will stand by you. I am prepared to die for this cause. Secondly, the present government is, even if not fully, a parliamentary government. We must trust it and support it. We need to make further efforts to communicate our will to the government and to see that it is acted upon. If the government does not stop the operation of the mine, I will not stop your action. I will stand by you and act with you. I will not lie. I will do what I promised you.

He expected the new government, which had just been formed under the leadership of Okuma and Itagaki, to do something since in its pronouncements it appeared to support the democratic rights of the people. Shozo made repeated appeals to the government leaders and at the Diet. But he could not succeed in his mission. He decided to resign from the Diet, and make a direct appeal to the emperor.

In 1902 Shozo was imprisoned for the fourth time, on charges of insulting a public officer. It was during this term of imprisonment that for the first time he read the Bible.

In 1904 the government decided to take over Yanaka village and to give assistance to those families which decided to move out. Tanaka went to the village. He decided to live there, in solidarity with the 16 families which did not leave. In 1907, the government ordered the destruction of the 16 houses. Shozo and the villagers took the case to the court.

Shozo died on 4 September 1913. In 1919, six years after his death, Yokyo district court decided in favour of the Yanaka village people.

All his life Shozo Tanaka waged a war against pollution, at a time when few people were aware of the problem. He was passionately committed to the protection of human life and the natural environment.

The starting point of his thought and action was the people in his local area. He wrote in his diary: "To destroy a village is to destroy the country." The struggle was between Yanaka village and the Ashio copper mine which was supported by the government. The people tried to defend the village even at the cost of their lives. For Shozo it was "a struggle to defend the constitution, our nature, and our ancestors", the struggle to defend one's *furusato*, the old village where people are born, live and die. It was his conviction that to destroy the people in the *furusato* was to destroy the state.

Repeatedly in his later years, he portrayed himself through the image of the ox which makes struggling steps along the muddy road:

> Beaten, buffeted
> By the rain and the wind,
> An ox drags his load
> Past, and is gone.
> Leaving only
> Wheel tracks in the mud
> And the sadness of things.[2]

---

[2] Translated by Kenneth Strong, *Ox Against Storm*, University of British Columbia Press, 1977, p.122.

Shozo's ethics

What are the ethical emphases that come through in his writings? All his life Shozo was concerned about the total wellbeing of the *furusato*. We can find four inter-related dimensions in his thought and action, four places or realms of life in which he found human responsibility.

1. The first is the dimension of nature, the realm of nature in which a human being is placed to fulfill his or her responsibility.

Shozo accepted and affirmed the cyclical rhythm of the four seasons as God's gift. For him the whole created cosmos was part of the inexhaustible treasure-house of God. Each season brought a fresh gift and joy.

> In spring man may go to the hills to view the blossoms, in summer to the open moors, in autumn to the hills to look at the fruits of the earth. When we see the autumn hills rejoicing in their dress of red maple leaves and white clouds, what need have we to dress ourselves in brilliant colours? An inexhaustible treasure-house of God's and our delight. The moon, the snow, the buds, and the blossoms, all are sources of this boundless joy we share with God, a joy that defies description by brush or tongue, for it is without end. What need have we to strive to accumulate other treasure than this?[3]

This sense of joy in the gifts of nature as the seasons unfailingly brought them is a mark of Japanese people. People respond to the uniqueness of the gifts of each season through the arts of cooking, flower arrangement, poetry, of *haiku* and *waka*, and the art of tea ceremony. This response to nature is the basis of Japanese culture. The old name of Japan is Yamato which means great harmony.

This understanding of nature was the background of Shozo Tanaka's decision to fight pollution. There is a

---

[3] *Ibid.*, p.219.

popular saying in Japan: "Even if the country experienced defeat, the river and the mountain remain constant." Shozo would have said: "If we destroy the mountain and the river, there is no country." He considered Japan as the *mizuho no kuni*, the country of abundant water and rice.

He wrote in his diary on 24 December 1912:

> To care for the mountain, your heart must be as a mountain.
> To care for the river, your heart must be as a river.

If one loses one's concern for the mountain, ultimately the tree will die. If trees die, the river will rise and flood the village. If the village is destroyed then the people will die. If people die, the country will also die. There is a cycle of cause and effect which we cannot escape.

Similarly he insisted that to govern the river one must cleanse one's heart:

> I often see people washing and rinsing their hands. Not their minds. They wash their faces, their bodies, their mouths, eyes, noses. But they are only the branches, not the root. So with the rivers. If a man thinks that merely clearing a river's passage and helping it flow is conservation, that is because he sees only the branches, and not the root; the root of river-care lies at the source, in the mountains, lakes, and forests. Caring for a river while neglecting the mountains is like a man who gorges himself on poison and dirt but pretends he is healthy and hygienic because he religiously washes and rinses his mouth.

Shozo firmly believed that the old village of Yanaka, with its river, fields, forest, and mountain, was a part of God's creation. It is the public responsibility of the farmer to cultivate the fields and to plant the crops. In opposition to the government officials who forced the people of Yanaka to move, Shozo said in 1908:

> If in their disgust with the people of Yanaka, the bureaucrats do not want them to cultivate the land, all right — let somebody else till the fields: Japanese, Americans,

Chinese, anyone. That the soil should be tilled is the law of
heaven. It does not matter if the Yanaka folk don't eat what's
grown there.

Let the birds eat the crops — the deer, the wild boar.
Heaven's laws would still be observed. Let thieves come
and steal the rice. Even that does not matter. That men and
animals should eat the fruits of the earth is heaven's law.
God would have none of them starve. Shozo does not say
it in so many words, but this understanding of the divine
law is quite biblical. It is the will of the biblical God to put
the human person in the garden to till it and keep it.

2. Then we note Shozo's relationship with his
neighbour. He became a neighbour to the victims of
pollution, the village people in Yanaka. He upheld the
right of self-government for the people of the village,
which is the basic unit of the nation. The starting point of
his thinking and action was from the bottom up, from the
rights of the people in the village, to the town, to the
prefecture, to the national government. He believed that
the responsibility of government officials is to serve the
people, but in actual fact they had become the slaves of
the mine owner.

Later on, in order to mobilize the people at the time of
the Second World War, the Japanese government used the
slogan: "Sacrifice self for the public need." In Shozo's
thinking the people were the first priority.

Jesus also emphasized the significance of those with no
status, the "least" (Matt. 25 and Luke 15). Shozo insisted
that "to destroy the least is to destroy the greatest". After
settling down in Yanaka village in 1904, Shozo came to
acknowledge a deeper understanding of the people.
Before that time he respected the rights of the people but
did not recognize their potential power. He went to protect
their rights, but he was not at that time aware of the power
of the people. Basically, he wanted only to help the people

59

whose rights were denied. As we put it today, in this instance the people were regarded as objects rather than subjects.

But once he immerses himself in the struggles of the people, there is a clearly discernible change in his attitude towards them.

> It is quite a normal thing that if people do not have enough food and clothes, they lose their good manners. It is rather extraordinary for people to maintain good manners when they go without food and clothes. Many of the poor in the village do not steal. Those who steal are the powerful. They take the property and the land of the people and are not afraid to kill the people with poison. It is rather a humbling experience to see many people, even in extreme poverty, who have not lost their personal integrity.

Shozo did not idolize the people. He knew well enough how poverty brings suffering and how the poor are weak and powerless. Yet now he recognized that this powerlessness is not without power. He wrote in a letter to a friend:

> Yanaka folk have little idea of their rights. They belong to an age long past. They are slow to anger when their dykes are destroyed, and even then they soon forget... They forget how it all happened. Peasants are earth. The earth is their "property", their food; they are like worms. But they are human too, though as different from merchants and businessmen as the earth from the sky.[4]

In 1909, six years after coming to Yanaka village, through living and struggling with the 16 families, some 100 people, left in the village, Shozo has a distinct change in his attitude. He wrote in his diary, 27 August 1907:

> This is the sixth year since I came to Yanaka village. I had thought that I did not learn anything. But this is a big

---

[4] *Ibid.*, p.182.

mistake... I discovered an extraordinary family among the ordinary village people. In the past five years I have come to know them very deeply... I was so stupid to search for God without paying attention to our neighbours who are so near to me. This is my mistake. For God is working among us and he is not necessarily far away. We must open our eyes to see the things around us, then we acknowledge the presence of God. If we search for God far away we do not find him. If we search for him near-by we can find him. The family of Yosaburo Somemiya is the messenger of God.

Yosaburo Somemiya was a man 50 years old, living in Yanaka with his wife, three daughters and two sons. Despite the hardship and suffering they experienced over the years, they maintained their basic goodness and simple kindness. They lived in a dilapidated house, but they were completely honest and unfailingly humane. There was little Shozo could add to the power of their integrity. He could no longer think of himself as the protector of the Yanaka people. He was their partner, sharing with them a life of struggle and hope.

An entry dated 23 January 1913 reads:

To learn from the ignorant seems a contradiction, the opposite of ordinary thinking. What is usual is to learn from the wise. It is human wisdom to learn from the wise. But it is heavenly wisdom to learn from the ignorant. There is an old saying about "learning from the bottom and communicating it to the top".

In relation to nature, Shozo was converted to return to the way of rivers and mountains. In relation to the people in Yanaka he was converted from seeing them as objects to be helped to affirming them as subjects who could shape their own history.

3. To be human means not only to live harmoniously with nature and to live as a partner with one's neighbour but also to live responsibly in relation to political power

and organization. Here Shozo Tanaka's life has much to teach us.

Shozo accepted the constitution as the basis of political participation. He did not use the term democracy but he firmly believed in the right of people to participate in decisions affecting their lives. He advocated the village as the basic unit of national life, convinced that it was the responsibility of the state to protect it. In the pollution issue he recognized the violation of this basic principle.

> To kill the people is to kill the nation.
> To despise the law is to despise the nation.
> This is the end of the nation.
> If its resources are abused, its people killed, and its laws overturned, no country can survive.[5]

In terms of his political thought, Shozo was not a radical anarchist but a constitutional monarchist. The Japanese people were in general loyal to the emperor. The problem was that some people used monarchy for wrong purposes.

> Our people's loyalty to their Emperor has no parallel throughout the world. But our rulers use this loyalty, as they use the whole polity of the nation — to serve their own power, and to put down the ordinary folk... The Restoration was carried out in the Emperor's name; but now evil subjects block the way, and that name is misused. Indeed, they use it now to destroy our nation, to kill our people...

One of the important contributions of Tanaka is his concept of the nation as the *family*. The Chinese characters which are used to denote the state mean national family. Shozo rightly pointed out that many of the changes which occurred in Japan were from the top downwards.

> It is in the nature of the Japanese social structure that change is from the top downwards, not the other way round.

---

[5] *Ibid.*, p.119; following two quotations: p.121, p.223.

Even "popular rights", and the constitution too, are handed down by officials, not demanded and appropriated by the people. It's strange. Japan is a constitutional monarchy and a robber state, both at the same time. I have nothing to do with "politics", nothing. For me Japan is a family. To care for rivers is to make sure that the garden is properly watered; to get rid of pollution is simple hygiene. This people do not understand. They call me a "politician" because they do not know the natural order of life in the family.

What he said is also true of the political changes which took place after the Second World War. Democracy was introduced and the peace constitution was enacted from the top downwards. Therefore, there is an urgent need to strengthen the people's democratic participation in the decision-making process.

Today we must widen the concept of the state as a national family to include all humankind, and work for the family of nations. Here Asia can make a significant contribution. Increasingly, people in contemporary Western society have lost the sense of the family as the basic unit of society. Instead they tend to opt for an individualistic or an organizational, bureaucratic way of life.

4. Shozo Tanaka found meaning and purpose in religious commitment. One of the chief obstacles we must surmount in our search for peace is our unquestioning commitment to the notion of national sovereignty. Japanese civil religion, national Shintoism, during the Second World War mobilized the people, demanding from them absolute loyalty to the nation. National security came to have top priority in the formulation of national policy and the preparation of the national budget. National sovereignty became the object of ultimate loyalty. Japan lost the war and it was indeed tragic to experience defeat. It was a humiliating experience. But I dare say it is not bad once in a while

to lose a war. By losing the war, we learned what we now accept, that the nation is a relative entity and not an absolute one.

We continue to consider national security the absolute goal of national policies. But in our interdependent world, no nation can survive by itself. The welfare of one nation is dependent on the welfare of other nations. We are living increasingly *in-between* the nations, in a family of nations.

Religion has a role to play in our quest for world peace precisely at this point. By constantly providing a transnational reference, religion can help us to see national security for what it is, an interim and relative value. It can give us the perspective to move towards a community of nations. The way to peace takes us on an eschatological journey; the journey will not end until the end of the world. In this journey we proceed one step at a time, with the vision of the heavenly city (the *heavenly furusato*). Then we should be able to see national sovereignty in the light of the sovereignty of God. Shozo Tanaka regarded the nation in terms of the national family. Limited as its importance is, it points in the right direction.

That was his source of hope amidst all his involvement in the affairs of the world. He was not a formal member of any religious institution. Nor was he a regular church-goer. But he was not irreligious. He was a humanist who rooted his life in religious convictions.

Since his boyhood he ardently studied Confucian ethics. He was well acquainted with the life and teachings of the Buddha. He disciplined himself daily by the Way of Heaven. But he experienced a radical change as he read the Bible for the first time. It was an experience of conversion. He came to recognize that what he was looking for could be found in the Bible. Shozo Tanaka was by no means a systematic theologian.

From fragments in his diary and letters we get glimpses of his biblical faith. For him the Bible was the basis of love and justice. He was not interested in ontological questions about God. But he sought spiritual grounding for action in relation to his suffering neighbours. Before he read the Bible, he affirmed the Heavenly Way, but he came to see this revealed in the life and work of Jesus Christ. He wrote in his diary on 31 March 1901: "If you want to be close to God, you must constantly read the Bible." He described his first encounter with the Bible:

> By the providence of God, I was in prison for 41 days in 1902. At that time I read the Bible and I became convinced that total disarmament is the way we should go.

He was profoundly impressed by the Beatitudes. Some of the verses he quotes in his diary and notes are revealing:

> Blessed are those who hunger and thirst for righteousness, Blessed are those who are persecuted for righteousness' sake. (Matt. 5:6, 10)
> If anyone strikes you on the right cheek, turn to him the other also. (Matt. 5:39)
> If any one forces you to go one mile, go with him two miles. (Matt. 5:41)
> Greater love has no man than this, that a man lay down his life for his friend (John 15:13)
> Man shall not live by bread alone. (Matt. 4:4)

It would be a mistake to think that Shozo reduced religion to ethics. No doubt he was passionately concerned with the power of religion to give direction and inspiration for action. But we should not overlook his strong recognition of the universal reality of human sin and of the need for salvation.

He believed that creation was good and beautiful. Through human corruption and selfishness it became evil and ugly. Salvation results from God's desire to restore the original beauty of all creation. Salvation was manifested in Christ who became the servant sacrificing himself on the cross. Repentance means to make the decisive turn, to accept the way of the cross and follow Christ. He wrote in his dairy, 1906:

> The physical destruction of Yanaka may not be far off now. I'm doing what little I can — it's the essence of religion — working for others: reborn themselves, they're trying to carve out a new way for the world.

Shozo Tanaka believed that religion gives the sustaining root for all human action. He became more interested in political involvement after coming to a religious commitment. With some people the more religious they become, the less "worldly" they are. In the case of Shozo the more religious he became the more he participated in the affairs of the world. His faith was the basis for his secular engagement.

We have already observed that he did not have any formal education in religion or theology, and that for the most part he studied by himself, reading religious books. Perhaps the only person Shozo regarded as a teacher was Osui Arai (1846-1922).

In 1870 Arai went to the United States with Arinori Mori, who later became the minister of education. Mori introduced Thomas Lake Harris to Arai. Under the influence of Harris, Arai joined a community called the Brotherhood of the New Life. He returned to Japan in 1899. He organized a small group called Kowa Sha and gathered a very limited number of disciples. Arai was not known widely until recently, but we are now beginning to acknowledge some of his unique approaches to Christianity.

He emphasized that religion was not to be known in the abstract; it is realized in concrete action in the world. For him Christianity was action-oriented; its essence was sharing in the life of Christ and living for others. Arai thought of and wrote about God not in terms of "Our Father", but as "Our Mother-Father", or "the Divine Man-Woman". This also influenced Shozo Tanaka. In his written prayer we also see him addressing God as "Our Father-Mother God!"

But how was it that the Bible and Jesus Christ meant more to Shozo than the religions he knew in Japan? He recognized the relevance of other faiths. Confucius was concerned over the ordering of political life. The Buddha's goal was to help people attain salvation through the mastery of the mind. Shozo respected these religious teachers. Yet he found in Christ unique characteristics. He believed God was in Christ manifesting God's love for the whole world and all humankind. Here is his testimony:

> Confucius devoted himself with sincerity to worldly affairs. Buddha went beyond worldly affairs and achieved Nirvana. Christ lived the truth. I follow Christ.

For him, God was in Christ taking the form of a person who embodied God's love and revealed its depth and comprehensiveness. He was impressed more by what Christ did than by what he taught.

Shozo recognized the fact that the traditional Japanese religions, through the long period of feudalism, had made people passive, acquiescent in the existing order and submissive to the ruling power. Religion in Japan tended to strengthen such characteristics as passive humility, formal order, and individual thrift. It stressed such virtues as inward piety, dependency, patience, forbearing, and humility. But he found among Christians many who dared to act according to what they believed. He wrote in his diary on 26 June 1911:

> Christians do not twist or change the biblical teaching. They express what has been taught consistently. Therefore they were often persecuted and not accepted by society. It is the characteristic of Christian religion to stand firmly by

what one believes, without making compromises… This (in turn) has also encouraged the Japanese Buddhist leaders to take up positive responsibility in the world…. Christians are a small minority in Japan but they have a wide impact, and they encourage people of other faiths by providing a concrete and living example of religion in society.

Shozo's Christian commitment resulted in a deep commitment to people. We have seen how the people of Yanaka became his teacher. He wrote:

God is in Yanaka. You yourselves are your Bible. Knowledge won through suffering is just as precious as the Bible. Books in themselves have no life! Read "The Book of Yanaka", then compare it with the Bible. Look back over what you have been through the last ten years, ponder it, learn it by heart — this is the way to discover a new truth. This is the way to heaven.

When Shozo says God is in Yanaka, he is not deifying the people of Yanaka; he is confessing that God is working in and through the suffering people of Yanaka. In enduring their hard life they exhibit something of the spirit of God. But they not only reflect the suffering of God but also witness to the power of the resurrection manifested in Christ. Following his teacher Arai, Shozo took seriously the reality of the resurrection which is a recurring experience in the midst of life.

For him resurrection was not a past event that happened 2000 years ago. It originates in Christ and it is happening in the cyclical life of the whole realm of creation through death and rebirth. Therefore he could speak often about the renewal of life in the midst of pollution and destruction.

Shozo never lost hope. It was his basic conviction that "if we do not know God there is no hope". But he who knows God can go forward with God.

As we saw there were two decisive events in the latter part of his life. At the age of 62, when he was in prison, he read the Bible for the first time and was converted to Christianity. Then at the age of 64, he decided to throw in his lot with the people of Yanaka village, and he lived with them until his death. These were the years of his Christian witness. He testified at the local court on 26 July 1912 that he believed in "the resurrection of self-government of the people". Behind that expression lay his religious conviction that the resurrection of Christ is our guarantee for the restoration of humanity. Shozo's hope for the future was not based on human factors; it was rooted in his faith in Immanuel, and God's raising Jesus from the dead.

Shozo was indeed a pioneer, not only in the anti-pollution movement but also in what we today call the people's movements which are organizations of suppressed people, struggling to achieve participation in the decision-making processes which affect their lives. He was a prophet pointing out the destructive consequences of industrialization and technological development.

Contemporary significance

Can Shozo's life help us in our study of Christian ethics in the Asian context?

The four dimensions of response we discern in him — nature, neighbour, nations and times — are important for us. They are inter-related, and must be taken as a whole. They are the places of response; they do not indicate a fixed order. Here I am closer to Dietrich Bonhoeffer who spoke of *mandate*, the entrusted places of responsibility, than to Emil Brunner who spoke of *order*. Bonhoeffer, as we have seen, identified the church, marriage and family, culture and government as the places of response or "divine mandates". I have rearranged the last three into two. The second of these represents human relationships within personal bonds, such as family, neighbourliness and friendship. The third represents our responsibility within what sociologists call the secondary organization, such as economic, social and political institutions. I used the term "between the times" to indicate our human responsibility in relation to religion or eternity. I have added the dimension of nature which I believe is crucially important. It is the universal calling of human beings to live in those four dimensions of life, making a proper response and maintaining an appropriate "betweenness" in each place. Since these four dimensions are universally applicable to all people, they may well provide a basis for comparative religious ethics.

The concept of "betweenness" contains a deep meaning in the Chinese character, 間. Although there are slightly different pronunciations, the basic meaning is shared not only by the Chinese people but also by Korean and Japanese people, a large number of Malaysians and the majority of people in Singapore and Hong Kong. They represent more than 1,400,000,000 people, about one-fourth of the total population of the world. (We take for granted that English is an almost universal language but actually those who use English as their native language are only about 265,095,000.)[6] The character for "betweenness" 間 indicates the basic ethical attitude of human life. That is to say, one person 人 is not human; one becomes a human 人 間 when one lives between nature, or space 空 間 ; between neighbours, 仲 間 ; between nations or worlds, 世間 ; and between the times, or history 時 間 . It is not accidental to have the character "betweenness" 間 in the expression of the basic four dimensions of human responsibility.

---

[6] *World Christian Encyclopedia*, Oxford University Press, 1982, p.10.

70

One appreciates space 空　間 when
One greets nature
One becomes human 人　間 when
One lives between neighbours 仲　間
One forms community when
One participates in the world 世　間
One creates history when
One lives between the times 時　間
If we do not have betweenness 間
We are no longer human
But fools, which means *manuke* 間　拔

Manuke literally means a person who is taken out of "betweenness".

4. Christ of Wabi

Let me return to the ha-hah approach vs the ya-yah approach, with which we began.

I said that when I participate in theological discussions I often sense an atmosphere of debate. This is particularly the case if there are Western participants taking part in the discussion. Then the approach is through rational arguments, and the attempt is to demolish other people's concepts of God. It is just like a theological *chanbara*, Japanese sword-fencing. I call that ya-yah theology since at the beginning of *chanbara* the participants shout a loud "ya-yah" after declaring their own name. In theology it is an approach of deductive metaphysics rather than inductive learning, an approach of confrontation rather than mutual sharing. What we need instead is the ha-hah approach, the approach of personal appreciation and mutual acknowledgment of what's going on in the living reality of life. This is close to the approach of artistic aspiration and response.

As a concrete example of the ha-hah approach from the Bible I would like to take the story of Jacob. Esau, his elder brother, was a strong and powerful hunter while Jacob had a slender body with a smooth skin. But he was a clever man. He deceived his father Isaac, and got the blessing of inheritance. Esau was understandably angry. Jacob fled to the desert. He took a stone for pillow, and went to sleep. It would have been a lonely and fearful experience to sleep alone in the desert.

He had a strange dream. He saw a ladder going up to heaven and angels ascending and descending on it. And he heard God's words of blessing: "I am with you and will keep you wherever you go." In the morning when Jacob awoke from his sleep he said to himself: "Surely the Lord is in this place, and I did not know it" (Gen. 28:10-17). It was a moment of surprised recognition. A vivid example of the ha-hah approach which discerns God's presence in the world and rejoices in it.

The relation between religion and culture

As we have already observed etymologically and historically there is an intimate relation between religion and culture.

Historically culture is related to the cultivation of the land as well as of the human personality. It involves the cultivation of one's whole body to enter into the proper relationship with an ultimate power. Religion and culture are intimately inter-related. While culture has to do with the cultivation of nature and person, religion cultivates the person directed towards an ultimate concern. As Paul Tillich said: "Religion is the substance of culture, and culture, the form of religion."[1]

The gospel is the message of salvation revealed in Jesus Christ and mediated through him. It works in and through various cultures, shaping and transforming them. The gospel is like a running stream of eternal water. Culture is like an earthly vessel that holds the water. The earthly vessel partakes of the unique local taste and colour — made of the local clay, utilizing the local tradition of craftsmanship. While the essence of the gospel is universal, the ways in which it is interpreted and expressed are uniquely local. Thus our key question is as to how we as Asian Christians, having cultural traditions and unique sensitivities, may interpret and express the Christian faith in an Asian context today.

A Christian reflection on *wabi*

It has been rather widely known that one of the characteristics of Japanese art is grasped in terms of *wabi* or *sabi*.

What is the central image used throughout the history of Western art to express the beautiful? One can say that it is

---

[1] *The Protestant Era*, Chicago, University of Chicago Press, 1948, p.57.

the body, the idealized human body. In one of Plato's Dialogues there is a discussion on beauty. One of the participants points out that the well-built body of a young man is the most beautiful thing in the world. The following conversation is recorded.

> Chaerephon called me (Socrates) and said: What do you think of him, Socrates? Has he not a beautiful face?
>
> Most beautiful, I said.
>
> But you would think nothing of his face, he replied, if you could see his naked form: he is absolutely perfect.
>
> And to this they all agreed.[2]

This idea of beauty was inherited by Michelangelo whose sculpture of David stands in Florence, Italy. Using this concern for the human body, the outstanding artist Botticelli depicted three beautiful nymphs to express the spirit of love. What was beautiful or adorable was expressed through the image of a beautiful female body. This was manifested at the time of the Renaissance through such images of the Holy Mother, the Annunciation and the Mona Lisa. We can see this trend throughout the history of Western art, and it persists. Beauty is expressed through the human body, either male or female.

In China, what is beautiful finds expression in the image of the dragon. A dragon is a mythological animal. Although it had no actual existence, it captured the popular imagination, and it was conceived as singularly powerful and always victorious. In the West dragons were regarded as heavy, evil and hideous; in China, the image of the dragon stood for something airy, benevolent, and powerful.

Kakuzo Okakura vividly describes the meaning of dragons in the East:

---

[2] B. Jowett, *The Dialogues of Plato*, New York, Random House, 1920, Vol. I, p.4.

74

The Eastern dragon is not the gruesome monster of
medieval imagination but the genius of strength and
goodness. He is the spirit of change, and therefore of life
itself. Hidden in the caverns of inaccessible mountains, or
coiled in the unfathomed depths of the sea, he awaits the
time when he slowly rouses himself into activity. He unfolds
himself in the storm clouds, washes his mane in the
blackness of the seething whirlpools. His claws are in the
fork of the lightning, his scales begin to glisten in the bark of
rain-swept pine trees. His voice is heard in the hurricane
which, scattering the withered leaves of the forest, quickens
a new spring.[3]

Thus we see the symbol of the dragon depicted
everywhere in Chinese royal palaces, from the thrones to
the emperors' garments, and from roof tiles to stone
decorations of walls. The influence of the tradition came
through Korea to Japan — so that even in the
contemporary culture of baseball teams we have a club
called Chunichi Dragons in the Central League in Japan.
   Similarly in Indonesia I believe the *garuda*, a mighty
mythological bird, is regarded as symbolizing strength
and speed and victory, like the dragon in China. In
Indonesian dramatic performances, at the most tense
moment of the struggle between good and evil, the *garuda*
often appears, bringing victory over the evil forces.
   What about Japan? What is thought of as beautiful in
Japan? How do Japanese people express what is beautiful?
According to Prof. Toyomune Minamoto, who taught
Japanese art history at the Kyoto University, something
worthy of adoration, an object of beauty, is the image of
autumn grasses. Not gorgeous flowers like roses or
magnolia, but the soft and tender flowering grasses in the
field. They are very tiny and fragile; they do not last for

---

[3] *The Awakening of Japan*, New York, Century Co., 1904, quoted by July
Allen and Jeanne Griffiths, *The Book of the Dragon*, London, Obis Publishing,
1979, p.34.

long. An ancient jar, excavated a few years ago, is decorated with a few simple, soft, tender lines depicting autumn grasses. In a picture story "book" (hand scroll) of the Heian Period (794-1185) we see similar soft lines combined with the calligraphy that tells the story.

Quite often they were painted not in colour but just with black ink on white paper. This is the unique philosophy of *sumie*, a black and white painting to express a colourful object through a non-colour technique. By restraining the colour, it expresses the vital essence of colour. There is indeed an

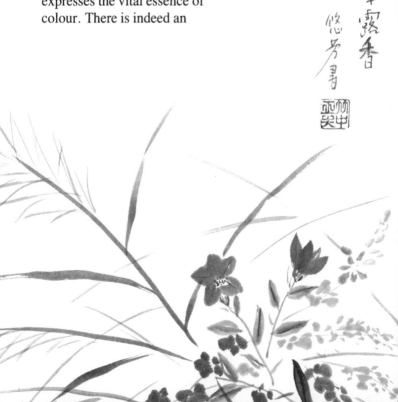

interesting correlation between artistic technique and philosophic aestheticism. By the elimination of colour, *sumie* tries to touch the colourful reality of the object. My painting guru repeatedly reminds me that there are five colours in *sumi*.

I may mention also in this connection the form of poetry *haiku*, which uses only 17 syllables, and is a sort of ascetic art or artistic asceticism.[4]

Let me touch on one more example of *wabi* before we analyze its relation to the Christian gospel.

After the Heian period we had the Momoyama period (1573-1615), which was known as a very colourful period. Leaders of the warrior class such as Oda Nobunaga and Toyotomi Hideyoshi were prominent figures of the period. They preferred gorgeous and colourful residences. In this period, the arrival of Portuguese missionaries and traders, coinciding with the colourful trend at home, brought colourful Western paintings and ornaments to Japan for the first time. Yet, against this background of the colourful Momoyama period, we see a sober non-colour style quietly permeating the scene. Between and to some extent overlapping the two colourful periods of Heian and Momoyama, there was the Kamakura period (1192-1333) in which Zen Buddhism took roots in Japan, emphasizing sober line with simplicity and a stern asceticism.

This was the time when the important art of tea was started by Rikyu (1522-1591), a tradition which continued to be maintained by each succeeding generation of his family. The grand tea master today is of the fifteenth generation.

Rikyu was a follower of Zen. He appreciated beauty in the simple, harmonious, sober life of everyday existence. Because of Rikyu's single-hearted concern for simple

---

4 R.H. Blyth, *History of Haiku*, Vol. 1, Tokyo, 1963.

beauty in the way of tea — and he was not supportive of the lavish external splendour of Hedeyoshi — he was ordered to perform self-immolation (*seppuku*). The way of tea was in sharp contrast to the colourful life of splendour and the gorgeous form of luxurious decorations which Hideyoshi, the warrior governor, preferred. Rikyu started a particular art of tea known as *wabi-cha*, the tea of *wabi*. It is the art of tea based on the spirit of *wabi*. According to Kakuzo Okakura, the author of the famous *Book of Tea, wabi-cha* is "a cult founded on the adoration of the beautiful among the sordid facts of everyday existence". *Wabi* is not just an artistic taste but it represents a way of living, a life of simplicity rather than luxury, a sober and restrained life rather than a life of ostentation. It appreciates the simple beauty in ordinary life rather than the colourfully decorated beauty in extraordinary surroundings.[5]

Wabi is beauty expressed without pretension, in a meek spirit and with harmony. It is not an abstract concept but a living reality contained in the simple atmosphere of a small tea room.

Historically the custom of drinking tea goes back to the Nara period (710-794). It gradually developed into a form of art, through the influence of Zen Buddhism during the Kamakura period. But the artistic style of the tea ceremony was formed in the Muromachi period (1392-1572). In this period, the tea ceremony was enjoyed by the members of the nobility and the upper classes. They not only tasted the cup of tea; they also appreciated the paintings and utensils, which often came from China. The whole process took place in a luxurious atmosphere. This kind of elaborate tea ceremony is called *shoin-chado* (the way of tea in the *shoin*, the study room), since they held

---

5 Fukutaro Nagashima, "Sen Rikyu", in *Chado Bunka Ronshu, Collected Essays on Cha-do*, Vol. II, 1982, p. 49f.

such a tea ceremony in the academic study rooms in the houses of nobility.

In contrast to the *shoin-chado* among the nobility in Kyoto, Rikyu emphasized *wabi-cha*, which was enjoyed by the ordinary merchants in Sakai, south of Osaka. It was held in a tiny room in a small building with a thatched roof. One comes into the small room by a narrow entrance called *nijiri*, itself a symbol of humility. Rikyu taught that a simple wild flower well displayed in a clean bamboo vessel was better than elaborate, colourful, cultivated flowers. He emphasized simplicity in all things connected with *wabi-cha*. Instead of using an expensive imported tea bowl, he used a black tea bowl made by one of his friends, Chojiro, an ordinary tile-maker. This indicated originally a simple celebration of beauty among the ordinary town people. As the tea ceremony increasingly becomes an elaborate cult, we need constantly to return to this original spirit.

The image of Christ — wabi in Christ

Wabi is one of the unique characteristics of the Japanese cultural tradition. It is not just a piece of art; it designates a way of life, a life of sober simplicity and humility. But how do we relate *wabi* to Christ? What is the image of Christ mediated from the cultural sensitivity which *wabi* represents? What are the unique characteristics — and limitations — of a *wabi* culture in the light of the Christian gospel? In order to pursue these questions, I want to focus our discussion on three issues which, I believe, are the important components of *wabi*: (1) a solitary life; (2) a life of poverty and simplicity; and (3) a life of emptiness and humility.

A solitary life

Jesus was not a solitary figure, alone and isolated from others. He was not preoccupied with himself. Far from it.

He was for the most part with his disciples and with people who were in need. He often participated in the celebrations of the village people and shared food and festivities with others — so much so that he was criticized by the Pharisees as a person "who eats and drinks with sinners and tax collectors" (Mark 2:16). Indeed this constant companionship with people is one of the important characteristics that we notice in the life of Jesus.[6]

Yet, we also find in the biblical record evidence of a solitary Christ, a Christ alone. From the beginning of his earthly journey, he has no place to stay.

> Foxes have holes, and birds of the air have nests, but the Son of Man has no place to lay his head. (Matt. 8:20)

Often he went to a quiet place to pray. But his life was not in opposition to his life of togetherness with the people. Rather, it was the source of his companionship with people. This is an important aspect in relation to the spirit of *wabi*.

The traditional Japanese concept of *wabi* more or less remained either in a closed circle or in isolation from the world. Yet in the *wabi* of Christ, or the biblical *wabi*, there is a rhythm between the solitary life and the life of worldly involvement. The more one is drawn to the transcendent life in solitude, the more one is called to live together with people in the world. One of the most agonizing aspects of a solitary life is to experience betrayal by a trusted person. Jesus experienced the deepest loneliness when he was betrayed by Judas, one of the trusted disciples, and when Peter denied him three times, the same Peter who confessed him as "the Christ, the son of the living God".

---

[6] See Shusaku Endo, *The Life of Jesus*, 1973.

A life of poverty and simplicity

The life of *wabi* is a life of simplicity. It sees beauty in
simplicity and in a disciplined life. Jesus was a poor man.
He was born in a manger and wrapped in swaddling
clothes. Quite often he and those of his company were
hungry (Matt. 21:18, Luke 6:1). They did not have enough
food. They did not own property. He was a man of *wabi*, a
man living in simplicity and serving the needs of the poor
and sick. One of his last admonitions to the disciples was
related to service to the least, with whom he identified
himself: those who were hungry, thirsty and those who
were strangers, sick, or in prison. Thus *wabi*, interpreted in
this way, is no longer concerned only with the welfare of a
closed circle: it provides a perspective to see realistically
the widening gap between the poor and the rich, and to
actualize justice and human rights in this world.

A life of emptiness and humility

Rikyu held up four values as important spiritual aspects
of the tea ceremony.
— Wa (harmony, peace)
— Kei (respect, appreciation)
— Sei (purity, cleanliness)
— Jyaku (tranquillity, emptiness)
Usually a tea ceremony takes place in a small room
which has an atmosphere of quiet and tranquillity. It is a
time of rest and quiet communion, with nature,
neighbours, and with the eternal power.

> Quiet reigns in the tea room, nothing breaks the silence
> save the sound of the boiling water in the iron kettle — the
> sound to the Japanese ear is like the sighing of pine trees on a
> distant mountain.[7]

---

[7] Toshihiko Izutsu, "The Elimination of Colour in Far Eastern Art and
Philosophy", in *Colour Symbolism*, Dallas, Texas, Spring Publications, 1977,
pp.175-76.

We may understand Christ better if we see him from the perspective of *wabi*. Often he kept silence. When the Pharisees brought to him a woman caught in adultery, Jesus bent down and wrote with his finger on the ground. We do not know what exactly he wrote. But we do know that he was silent. That silence is full of meaning. In the home of Lazarus, exposed to the deep grief of his friends, he wept. "When Jesus saw her weeping, and the Jews who came with her also weeping, he was deeply moved in spirit and troubled — Jesus wept" (John 11:33-35). The tears of Jesus were an expression of concern and sympathy, and of identification.

In the garden of Gethsemane, he prayed in agony of the spirit: "My Father, if it be possible, let this cup pass from me; nevertheless, not as I will, but as you will" (Matt. 26:39).

We recall the words of Paul:

> Have this mind among yourselves, which you have in Christ Jesus, who, though he was in the form of God, did not count equality with God a thing to be grasped, but emptied himself, taking the form of a servant, being born in the likeness of men. And being found in human form he humbled himself and became obedient to death, even death on a cross. (Phil. 2:5-8)

Here we find the concept of *wabi*, in terms of self-emptiness, concretely actualized in the person of Jesus Christ. *Wabi* is no longer an ideal state of life we search for; it is revealed in history on the cross. And as in *wabi-cha* there is a taste of bitterness.

Professor Tadakazu Uwoki, who used to teach the history of Christian thought at the School of Theology in Doshisha University, encouraged the development of a Christian koinonia, fellowship through the tea ceremony. He helped to form a group called Migiwa-kai (the fellowship beside still waters) among those

Christians who were interested in the tea ceremony. He formulated the following nine articles to indicate a Christian expression of the meaning of the tea ceremony.

The spirit in which to share a tea-koinonia

1. Christ loved the household of Mary and Martha and enjoyed their friendship and the relaxed family atmosphere. It is an invitation to us to share a cup of tea (Luke 10:38-42).

2. One of the blessings of the tea ceremony is that it enables us to appreciate the gifts of nature. This reminds us of the teachings of Christ, especially of those where he refers to the flowers in the field and the birds of the air (Matt. 6:26-30).

3. The circle of friendship in the tea room reminds us of the fellowship of two or three gathered together in his name (Matt 18:20).

4. Informal ritual and warm fellowship reflect the beauty of the communion of the saints (Ps. 133).

5. The attentive concern to find goodness in incompleteness reminds us of his grace in forgiving the sinner (1 Cor. 1:26-31).

6. It reminds us how God can bring an abundant life out of poverty (2 Cor. 6:10).

7. The taste of bitter tea helps us to understand grace in the midst of suffering (Matt. 26:39).

8. The master of the tea ceremony trains him- or herself in the art of tea through the way of servanthood (Rom. 5:3-5).

9. Here in the tea ceremony there is no formal teaching, only a mutual sharing, a joyful discipline, and life with a formal arrangement (John 3:7-8).

Let me conclude with two poems concerning bamboo. The first is of traditional Chinese origin and the other is my own composition.

Even if you do not have beef on the table
You must have a bamboo in your house
If you do not have beef on the table
You will become a little bit thin
But if you do not have bamboo you will be
    corrupted
It is difficult to cure a corrupted man

The meaning of *wabi* is illustrated
through the image of bamboo:

Bamboo grove — a clean wind comes and goes
Bamboo leaves eternally green
Bamboo roots continuously stretching
    in solidarity
The Bamboo centre shows emptiness.